Praise

Stressed to Splessed isn't just a guide—it's a revelation. I initially sought this book as a resource for others, but it quickly became a favorite reference, showing me that true peace is possible, even in the face of life's greatest challenges. The eight-part journey is more than a series of steps; it's a Spirit-led roadmap to lasting transformation.

—Niccie Kliegl
Founder, Fulfill Your Legacy; author, speaker, coach

Susan is marked by maturity and wisdom that has been refined through the crucible of suffering. Her story and the principles she draws from it reflect a wonderful blend of honesty, humility, and humor as she gives glory to God for the work in her life. This book provides biblical truth to help orient your perspective and a hope-filled outlook to encourage your heart.

—Dr. Tiam Cochrell
Pastor, Grace Baptist Church

I have had the privilege of knowing and loving Susan all of her life, and if she was introducing me she would quickly say I am the older sister and she is the younger! She has always had a wonderful sense of humor! Susan has written a book that not only exposes her pain, heartache, and grief, but also provides hope and passage through those hard times. *Stressed to Splessed* is a book you will pick up multiple times, and each time gain new understanding and wisdom on how to move from "stressed to splessed."

—Carolyn Macdonal
Retired high school teacher

Stressed to Splessed encouraged me greatly, and I highly recommend it to anyone who has ever experienced trauma or hardship. Prof. Troth, as her students love to call her, provides a loving and positive influence in our lives. She lives out the principles written in this book daily and allows God to use every trial in her life for His glory. This book uplifted my heart, and I think it will uplift yours too!

—Rachel White
Cedarville University Class of 2026

Susan and I both share a love of music, especially singing as we are both vocal coaches. We also share in the experience of grief and loss. In this perfectly sized book, you'll find practical ways to work through your grief and move into the new place God has for you. Through witty and often touching stories about her own life and the lives of others, you'll find yourself relating to their pain and rejoicing in the hope that's offered. I pray that this vulnerable offering of love and insights helps you on your way to total healing and a "splessed" future.

—Sherri Gould
Vocal coach

I have known Susan Troth for several years as a colleague at Cedarville University. And we've had the opportunity to work on a number of things together, both on campus and our local church. In the years that I've known her, I have seen her walk through some difficult, stressful times, and yet I have always seen her praising the Lord. So when she approached me and shared about a book discussing how stress can turn to blessings, my first thought was "That is so Susan!" But as I thought about it, I realized "No, it's not 'That's so Susan'—it is 'That's so *God*!'"

I trust that as you read this book, you will be challenged and encouraged at how God can take stresses in our lives and turn them into His blessings. Susan is truly "splessed," and I am grateful that she is sharing God's blessings with us. May we *all* experience the splessing of God as we let Susan's life encourage us in our own walk.

—Jeff Beste

Director of Development, Cedarville University

Stressed to Splessed

A faith-based journey to find
healing, hope, and new horizons

SUSAN C. TROTH

BRIGHT
INK
PRESS

2024 First Edition
Ebook ISBN - 978-1-965905-08-1
Paperback ISBN - 978-1-965905-01-2
Hardcover ISBN - 978-1-965905-00-5

Published by Bright Ink Press
12 Boulevard, Tallapoosa, GA 30176

Dedication

To Abba, my Heavenly Father, who is infinitely patient and tender with me; to the Cowboy who was sent to love and encourage me (Rick); to my bonus children who cheer me on; to Cacky who is the best big sister, and our brother Bubba; to my family—Troths, Williams and Plemons; to my Cedarville University family; to Niccie, the best coach; and to my prayer partners Jackie and Deb—my love, gratitude, and devotion to you all.

Table of Contents

Forward

by Dwayne Moore

In the story of our lives, there is a foreword that has already been written by the Author and Finisher of our faith. Before the foundation of the world, we were in his mind and on his heart. In Psalm 139:16 (NLT), David writes, "You saw me before I was born. Every day of my life was recorded in your book. Every moment was laid out before a single day had passed."

In the opening pages of this book, Susan writes, "When we define ourselves in Christ then that definition doesn't change, even when circumstances do." She goes on to share some incredible insights she's learned about who she is in God's eyes. Here are a few of my favorites from her list:

- I am God's workmanship created in Christ Jesus to do good works.
- I am brought near through the blood of Jesus.
- I am built on the foundation with Christ as the cornerstone.
- I am a cracked pot of clay who is loved by the Potter.

Susan masterfully weaves biblical promises throughout this book. As you pour through its pages, I encourage you to allow those truths to pour over you and remind you of the loving foreword God has already written for you.

Forward

This book is about moving forward—or as Paul put it, "forgetting what lies behind and straining forward to what lies ahead" (Philippians 3:13b). Despite his circumstances, that is what Paul did. And, as you read her story, you'll discover that's what Susan did as well. By God's grace, she moved forward.

Susan goes into stark detail about some of her darkest moments in life. Few of us would want to experience the kind of challenges and trials she has been through. Losing her husband, not being able to have children, almost dying from renal failure and RSV: these are the sort of things that stunt many people emotionally and cause them to stop moving ahead and progressing in life. But not Susan. She turned her trials into triumphs. When she was at her lowest point, she did what we all need to do. In her words, "I surrendered. And the peace that passes understanding began to flood my soul."

I met Susan at a ministry conference in 2019. It had been almost two years since her husband had died. She told me of his passing when we met, but I didn't realize how deep and dark a valley she was still in—not until I read the manuscript of this book, in fact. In her words, it was in 2019 when she was "actually totally alone." I would have never guessed she felt that way then. She smiled when she spoke; she was filled with joy, and her words and countenance showed that she clearly had hope. She got excited hearing about the mission opportunities our ministry leads around the world, and she immediately wanted more information. She wanted to know how her students at Cedarville University could get involved.

Interestingly, she didn't dominate our conversation by talking about her past. Her mind was focused more on the future and on helping others. Some might hear this and think perhaps she just "hid it well." I don't think so. She wasn't hiding her feelings, and she wasn't faking anything. On the contrary, she was letting the peace of Christ rule in her heart, and it showed.

Four Words

When I read this book, four words come to mind: wisdom, intrigue, truth, and hope.

Wisdom

I've heard it said that experience brings wisdom, but that's not quite accurate. True wisdom comes from God and from searching his Word. *Stressed to Splessed* is filled with solid wisdom because it is filled with Scripture. This book is replete with powerful references to Bible passages and how to apply them in our daily lives.

Intrigue

Susan is a natural storyteller. The detailed and sometimes harrowing accounts she shares are sure to keep your interest and pique your curiosity. You may even find that this is a book you can't put down. Each chapter is a poignant reminder of God's grace and mercy and of our great need of him.

Truth

Jesus said, "you will know the truth, and the truth will set you free" (John 8:32). Susan devotes an entire chapter to the importance of truth. Through her own story in this book and through the stories of others that she invited to share, the reader is challenged: "Be careful who you listen to. Lean into God and let Him guide."

Hope

If I were to sum this book up in one word, it would be "hope." Whether you need hope or have someone in your life who needs hope, these chapters are for you. You'll not only gain hope, but you'll also learn how to share real hope. Susan defines hope with an acrostic that's golden. Honestly, I'd buy the book just for that. But I won't spoil it for you here. You'll need to read almost to the end to discover what it stands for.

You might notice that with these four words—wisdom, intrigue, truth, and hope—I made an acrostic of my own. So, in closing, I'll say: sit down *with* this book. Walk along with Susan. And never doubt again that God is with you and for you.

Dwayne Moore
Author and founder, Next Level Worship International

Forward

by Dr. Edna Frenchwood

Stress, pain, hopelessness, forgiveness, and hope—these are themes that resonate deeply with women all over the world. *Stressed to Splessed* masterfully captures the emotional and spiritual journey from despair to redemption through Christ in a world that often confronts us with immense trials. As you open the pages of this book, you will embark on a journey that mirrors the heartache, longing, and ultimate healing that so many women experience, reminding us of the power of faith and the love of Christ that holds us even in our darkest moments.

The beauty of this novel lies in its raw portrayal of human suffering and the complexities of a broken world. Pain is an inevitable part of life, and for many, it manifests in various forms—emotional trauma, physical suffering, relational brokenness, or spiritual despair. Psalm 34:18 (NIV) states: "The LORD is close to the brokenhearted and saves those who are crushed in spirit." Susan does not shy away from exposing these deep wounds. Instead, she paints a vivid picture of what it looks like to be in the trenches of hurt and hopelessness, where the light seems dim and the way forward appears uncertain.

Yet, as readers will quickly discover, this is not a story of defeat. This book beautifully illustrates how, amid this pain, there is a divine invitation to something greater. This is a familiar yet often elusive truth for all women: Christ invites us to meet Him in our suffering. The cross itself is a testament to this—He bore our pain so that we might have hope. But how do we, as modern women, live out this reality when life feels overwhelming? Well, we need to move from "stressed to splessed." Susan teaches us how to do so!

Stressed to Splessed provides an answer. Through the story of Susan who, much like many of us, battles with grief, bitterness, and a sense of abandonment, we witness the transformative power of forgiveness. Forgiveness is not presented as an easy, surface-level decision but as a soul-deep process that requires vulnerability and divine strength. For women, especially those who have endured deep personal hurt, the concept of forgiveness can seem like an impossible feat. But as Romans 8:18 (NIV) states, "I consider that the sufferings of this present time are not worth comparing with the glory that is to be revealed to us." In all this, Susan delicately navigates this topic, offering a Christ-centered perspective that shows forgiveness not as something we muster up ourselves but as a grace that flows from Jesus.

For the Christian woman, this message is crucial. We live in a world that encourages self-reliance and sometimes even justifies holding on to anger or hurt. When she writes about anger toward God, we all can relate. But the gospel calls us to something higher—to release the weight of our pain to God, and trust that His justice and love are greater than any hurt we carry. This book serves as a gentle yet powerful reminder that we are not meant to carry the burden of bitterness. Instead, through Christ, we are invited to let go and, in turn, find healing and freedom.

This book also touches on the profound concept of hope—hope that is not based on our circumstances but is anchored in Christ. One of the most powerful moments in the story is when Susan realizes that her circumstances, though painful, are not the end of her story. This realization leads her to a deeper understanding of Christ and the hope He offers. This is the turning point, not just for Susan but for the reader as well. At this moment we, as women, are reminded that no matter how bleak our situation may seem, hope in Christ never fails. His promises are eternal, and He walks with us every step of the way.

For women today, many of whom face pressure to keep up appearances, and manage careers, families, and faith, this novel is a much-needed reminder to pause, reflect, and seek Christ deeply. Susan's journey toward spiritual renewal serves as an invitation for all readers to pursue a deeper walk with Christ. It is a call to surrender—not in weakness, but in strength, knowing that God's plans are always greater than our own. As Psalm 147:3 states, "He heals the brokenhearted and binds up their wounds."

As you read this book, I hope you allow yourself to connect with Susan and her purpose for this book. I pray you have an open heart about your story and where God is taking you. I encourage you to seek his face for answers that bring light to your world and others around you. "You are the light of the world" (Matthew 5:14)! As Susan has taught us, I hope you remind yourself that you and your journey are splessed always!

Edna Frenchwood

Dr. Frenchwood is a goodwill ambassador to the state of Georgia. She is a recipient of the US Presidential Lifetime Achievement Award and personal publicist to senators, commissioners, and kings.

Preface

There is a divine beauty in brokenness. In those moments when life overwhelms us—when the weight of stress, loss, and pain feel too heavy to carry—it is easy to believe that we are alone. But the truth is, we are never alone. Even in the darkest valleys, there is a light that guides us, a hand that reaches out to lift us up, and a hope that waits to be discovered.

This book, *Stressed to Splessed*, is born out of that truth. It is more than just words on a page—it is an invitation. An invitation to step into a sacred journey where healing is possible, hope is restored, and new horizons are in sight. For every woman who has found herself overwhelmed by the pressures of life, for every heart weighed down by grief, this book offers a path forward.

I have had the honor of seeing women just like you move from feeling trapped in the shadows of their struggles to standing in the light of healing and freedom. I believe that is possible for you too. Whether you are in the beginning stages of your grief, in the messy middle, or nearing the end of a long season of struggle, there is hope on the other side. And through this journey, you will not only find healing—you will find yourself being gently held and lovingly led by the God who has never left your side.

So, my dear sister, as you open these pages, take a deep breath. You are about to embark on a beautiful transformation. Each chapter, each step, is a part of the masterpiece God is creating in your life. Through the tears, there is triumph. From the stressed there emerges "splessed." And as you walk this journey, you will discover that stress is not the end of your story—it is the beginning of your healing.

Let this journey be the pathway that leads you to healing, hope, and new horizons.

With love and anticipation for your transformation,
Susan C. Troth

Introduction

I wasn't even sixty years old. I'd been through infertility, tough years of ministry, widowhood, and almost died—but people would ask me how I was and I would just blurt out . . . *"Splessed."* Who does that?

It doesn't make sense.
I shouldn't be joyful.
It's crazy that I'm so peaceful.
Even crazier that I don't dwell in regrets.
Amazing that I'm not bitter/jealous.

How can I be grateful to God for my life? Why do I feel beyond blessed, to cup running over, spoiled and . . . splessed?

It made me think: How did I get here?

I don't understand God's ways. He is God, and I will never fully understand Him. I don't understand why He gave me so much and yet didn't give me my biggest heart's desire for children. I don't understand why I was widowed at 55—alone in Ohio with no children and no family living near me. I don't understand why, just after I felt healed and ready to move forward, God allowed me to go to the brink of death. I just don't understand. I think there might be other women out there who struggle with understanding, acceptance, and being happy with their journey. That's why I'm sharing. I hope you will find tools that will lead you to the splessed life that I have found.

Who am I?

There were key indicators of how God had shaped my life from a very early age. When I was little I sang "Standing on the Promises" while looking in the mirror (oh, the performer's ego). When I was three, I wouldn't allow my preschool choir to sing in church until I had properly organized them on the stage (a choral conductor was born).

It took an incredibly lonely birthday (actually totally alone in 2019), with much weeping and I'm sure consuming of sugary products, to deeply wrestle with God about my identity. I could tell who I wasn't—a wife anymore, a mom, a minister's wife. I could tell you my job—musician. But I hadn't learned to define myself in Christ, rather than on outward circumstances. You see, when we define ourselves in Christ. that definition doesn't change, even when circumstances do. Even now, when a small voice whispers, "What are you doing, writing a book? You are a musician." Even now—I have to remind myself who I am . . .

So—who am I? Check out the paper on my bathroom mirror, where I collected what I learned from the book of Ephesians:

- I am blessed with every spiritual blessing in Christ.
- I am chosen in Him before the creation of the world.
- I am predestined to be adopted.
- I am redeemed and forgiven.
- I am to be for the praise of his glory.
- I am sealed with the Holy Spirit—God's possession.
- I have hope—his glorious inheritance.
- I have his incomparably great power.
- I am alive with Christ.
- I am God's workmanship (poem) created in Christ

Jesus to do good works which God prepared in advance for me to do.

- I am brought near through the blood of Jesus and have access to the Father through Jesus.
- I am a fellow citizen, a member of God's household.
- I am built on the foundation with Christ as the cornerstone to become a dwelling in which God lives by His Spirit.
- I am a cracked pot of clay who is loved by the Potter.

In my years of walking alongside those navigating pain and loss, I've witnessed how transformative the journey of restoration can be when we partner with God. This is not a journey you walk alone. The steps laid out in the S.P.L.E.S.S.E.D. process—a journey of surrender; prayer; leaning into truth; embracing emotions; listening for the still, small voice; enduring through the work; discovering hope; and stepping into new horizons—are designed to gently guide you from a place of stress and heartache to a place of peace, purpose, and God-given restoration.

In this book I'm going to start by sharing the major cracks in my life, to help you understand that even the broken pieces are used by the Potter to make our pots beautiful. Then I'm going to share how I grew to live a splessed life, as well as stories from others who are living splessed, as well.

What is "splessed"?

Beyond blessed. . . . My cup runs over . . . so blessed, I feel spoiled . . . despite hurts, cracks in the pot, suffering, death, the valleys of life.

How did I find it?

I lift up my eyes to the hills,
Where does my help come from?
My help comes from the LORD,
who made heaven and earth.

He will not let your foot be moved;
He who keeps you will not slumber.
Behold, he who keeps Israel
will neither slumber nor sleep.

The LORD is your keeper;
The LORD is your shade on your right hand.
The sun shall not strike you by day,
nor the moon by night.

The LORD will keep you from all evil;
He will keep your life.
The LORD will keep
your going out and your coming in
from this time forth and forevermore.
(Psalm 121)

PART I
Stressed

CHAPTER ONE

Barren County

Barren.

It is a kick in the gut. I hate that word, but I can't escape it.

The picture is bleak but accurate: desolate landscape, lonely existence, without life.

I've lived in Ohio for seventeen years and have probably driven more than fifty times to see my sister in Nashville. Each time, I drive through Barren County, Kentucky ... I wince. It still hurts. Barren. That's a tough word for me to even type. I have a trick where I've learned to squeeze my legs so I don't cry around people and I'm doing it now, so I don't upset the apple cart in this peaceful home where I'm working. But it still triggers.

My first husband, Dr. Ron Plemons, and I were married December 21, 1984. I went to see my gynecologist shortly before the big date for a routine checkup and the results were upsetting, to say the least. The doctor informed me that I had endometriosis and it might be difficult to get pregnant. I told Ronney that he was absolutely free to walk away from the wedding and he said no: "We will go through this together."

I'll fast-forward through Ronney's years in Bible college and seminary to when we went to our first church—Southside Baptist in Lakeland, Florida. In God's mercy, it was a church

1

that I had attended for three years as a teen; I still had friends and my brother's family in the church as well as my parents an hour away. God put me in the midst of a support system, because He knew how tough life was going to get—He leads me (Psalm 23).

With Ronney out of seminary we really leaned into trying to start a family. My OB-GYN sent me to a fertility specialist in Orlando. It's hard to remember all the procedures we had to do; I've probably blocked out most of it. But it was a rollercoaster, both emotionally and physically. I had surgery, tests, probing, shots, and drugs that took me through menopause (yes, I've had two rounds of menopause!). In addition, the doctor told me that my womb was too weak to carry more than one child so that if I did get pregnant with twins he would want to abort one. We wouldn't abort. It was scary.

Then there was the added stress of going through this while in the ministry. Being the senior pastor puts your life in a fishbowl. Most of the congregants want to know your business, and many like to discuss your life. A few would catch me at church just to give me advice on how to get pregnant—not a conversation I wanted to have. It began to get incredibly difficult to attend baby showers and watch my family and friends enjoy their children. Mother's Day is still the most painful day of the year, and I usually had to endure it at the front of the church in the choir or sitting at the piano, in the most visible place, while I squeezed my body so I wouldn't cry.

Nine years later we heard, "I don't know why you aren't getting pregnant. There is nothing else I can do except in vitro fertilization." Ronney and I had already determined that we didn't have the finances to do in vitro, and that even if we did, we did not want to leave frozen embryos on the shelf; also, my weak womb would make multiple babies and attempts difficult. Someone offered to pay for it. We said,

"No, thanks."

Barren County.

We didn't understand. I was shocked. We had already figured out the names—Timothy Gerald and Madison Suzanne. We had bought cute baby outfits and accessories and put them in a hope chest. Most of them are still there. Until now, most people didn't know about the hope chest for my babies and our names. God knew.

It still hurts. Deeply. I still ache. Like now. Gotta pause.

God moved us to a church in Houston in 2000. It was a bitter and sweet good-bye. It was there that I began to lean into other options. I had already brought up adoption, but Ronney wouldn't consider it or talk about it. I think he was hurting too much and was incredibly worried about our finances because insurance didn't cover any of the infertility treatments. We were six figures in debt. But I was desperate to be a mom, so I wanted to spend yet more money to adopt. We also began to get training to become foster parents.

To say that it strained our relationship would be an understatement. I know couples that have divorced because of infertility. But we soldiered on and found our way. We leaned into ministry

We began to seek out opportunities to be spiritual parents to our nieces and nephews. Sometimes this meant inviting them to dinner to have intentional conversations about the directions of their lives and sometimes it meant living with us for a summer. We also became "godparents" to Abbey, whose parents had become close friends and asked us to look after her should it ever be needed. What a joy to be a part of their family and to watch her grow into a godly young woman.

We began to seek out opportunities to be spiritual parents.

My happiest year as a spiritual mom was when we had a German exchange student in our home. I had thought often about hosting exchange students, but somehow I sensed that the time was right and there was a family in our church that helped to organize the local program. I asked Ronney, and he said yes to a young man from Germany. God showed up in surprising way.

Before that, I had lost my job. It was devastating. I loved my job as a music teacher for a local high school—three hundred students a day to love and nurture. I didn't understand it. Then a local Christian university asked me to adjunct-teach voice part-time. In hindsight, God allowed this for several reasons, including the fact that I had so much more time to be a mom that year. The soccer practices, the youth group events, the "taxi service"—what a joy to experience it. Nico was a fixture at church and a popular soccer player at Fairborn High School. I was in domestic heaven.

Second, you would have assumed that Nico was Ronney's son. They looked alike and even acted alike. We bonded. For his sixteenth birthday we took him to Washington, DC to tour the White House, and to visit the Smithsonian and Mount Vernon. I couldn't get over how he liked to read all of the exhibit information just like Ronney. Nico began to call us his "'Merican Mom and Dad." It was so tough to send him back home, a dark day for all of us. But we still stay in touch.

I have been such a splessed spiritual mom and have experienced so many wonderful things through these families. I was able to help Ronney's niece, Bria, plan her wedding. Nico was a groomsman for his friend's wedding, and then there was Abbey's wedding in which I was able to be part of the family. It is not how I imagined these things would happen, but I am so grateful.

4

CHAPTER TWO

Meanistry

W e were both so naive when we stepped into God's calling on our lives to serve His church. God doesn't love us or call us because we are perfect. In fact, we are all imperfect and full of mistakes, but He loves us. That is such a soothing thought. I will never be good enough and I don't ever have to be good enough for God's love. He knows all of my faults and still loves me.

In 1982, when I was at Baylor University and changed my major from music education to church music, I was totally unaware of the controversy it would bring. I didn't have a political or feminist agenda; I just wanted to use music in the church.

Ronney was saved while in college and within the year he had surrendered to full-time ministry. He hadn't grown up in church—in fact, he read the Bible and compared denominations to find the one that he believed most reflected the truth found in God's Word. And that's what he joined: a Southern Baptist church.

We served the church together as pastor and minister of music/worship for thirteen years. Before and after I "retired" from ministry, I served the church as the wife of a youth pastor and senior pastor. Thirty-one years of ministry. Lots of scars.

As they say, "Hurt people hurt people." Everyone in the church has been scarred by sin and most carry deep hurts. Some attack the church leadership with those hurts, to put it mildly. Some attack the ministry families. There were some who attacked us in business meetings, Sunday School classes, church hallways, to our faces, and behind our backs (but it usually found its way to our ears). We even had a couple who stood in our driveway and said, "We love you" in May and in October called for Ronney's firing because he had made a decision they didn't like.

Why do ministers do it? Because it is our calling, our job. Because we reflect God's love for his sheep—despite our imperfections. We do it because we are addicted to seeing the love of God change people's lives, as I saw in the Facebook message I received a few months ago:

> Susan. I don't know if you remember coming to my house and presenting the gospel to me, but I remember it greatly. I truly appreciate you walking out in faith and opening my eyes to Jesus. Thank you. Know that my time at Cornerstone was truly special to me. I matured greatly, found my wife, my calling, and found myself in Christ, and you will always hold a special place in my heart because of it. God Bless.

It is saved on my phone.

I thought the church would appreciate all the extra time I gave to serve, since we didn't have children. But mostly, the church just didn't like the fact that we didn't have children. It was a barrier to us connecting with families. It was thrown back in our faces, a source of jabs from the women in the church. One Sunday I was literally asked, in front of a senior adult women's Sunday School class, why I had such a pouch of a stomach since I had never had children.

I went home and cried.

6

We need to see each other's flaws and not quit.

How incredibly mean and insensitive we can be. There are toxic people in the church. I don't need to share all the stories. There are hurting people in the church. There are also loving, godly people in the church.

God's Word doesn't tell us to attend church because it is easy, but because we will be sharpened like iron sharpens iron. It is where we learn how to function as a Christian family. It is through tough times and challenges that we learn how to be strong and endure. We need this endurance for jobs, marriages, families, friendships—all of life. We need to see each other's flaws and not quit. Almost every day I hear about families who no longer speak to each other and people who walk away from churches, jobs, friendships, and families because they get hurt. That's not love. Love sacrifices and forgives. Just look at Jesus on the cross for my sins.

I don't want to dump all of the hurts here. It still hurts sometimes. But I'm glad that we served.

The saying is trustworthy and deserving of full acceptance, that Christ Jesus came into the world to save sinners, of whom I am the foremost.

(1 Timothy 1:15—Ronney's favorite scripture)

CHAPTER THREE

Widow

Precious in the sight of the LORD is the death of his saints.
(Psalm 116:15)

I remember living in Houston and opening a letter from a church in Ohio that said they had Ronney's resume and that he was a top candidate for their senior pastor position. I laughed. I almost threw it away. I showed it to Ronney, and we put it in the back of our minds. We had sensed God's prompting that He was going to move us, and we wanted to serve outside of the Bible Belt. The Midwest sounded good, but—Fairborn, Ohio? Little did we know.

The mortgage on our home had become unbearable due to tax increases and the market in Houston was flooded with new home builds, so we decided to put our house up for sale, since there was no rush. It sold in three weeks. We didn't know God's timing for moving us to a new pasture and buying a house short-term was not wise, so we found an apartment close to the church. Then Hurricane Katrina hit New Orleans, and refugees began to pour into Houston. Apartments were scarce and we hadn't signed a lease on the one that we found.

We moved into a lower-income apartment complex. We had gone from a new middle-class home where we

9

hosted dinners and parties and enjoyed the wild peacock in our neighborhood; to an upstairs apartment in a sketchy complex—robberies, break-ins, drugs.

We began to walk the dog and meet the neighbors. One told me that I was his first white friend. I don't know about that, but I do know that God taught me the importance of building relationships during this time. The connection might be dogs, music, or sports, but God can use those connections to open the door to ministry. Sometimes the ministry was listening and praying. Sometimes it was food or fun. The seeds of Jesus' love can be sown in any ground.

A year and a half later, in 2007, we moved to Fairborn. God's ways are not our ways, and His timing is usually not our timing. But it is always perfect, though we might not see it now. I learned about waiting on God as we lived in our apartment.

One year later Ronney just couldn't shake a bad cold. He went to see our family doctor and the EKG didn't look good. The doctor tried to call an ambulance, but Ronney wanted me to drive him so we headed to the hospital. Waiting for test results was, to put it mildly, tough. I can't remember all of them—enzymes, angiogram—but the results were not good. I remember standing in the hall after the angiogram and the doctor told me that he could hardly find a healthy artery. I just leaned against the cold wall and sobbed. How could this be happening?

The results of testing were quadruple heart bypass surgery, and the surgeon told me that it was difficult to find any good veins in Ronney's legs for the procedure. He had the same disease as his father, coronary heart disease, in which the arterial system throughout his body was being blocked. He was only 46.

Life changes so quickly.

I remember so much stress and tears and fear.

I also remember God moments. . . .

Dr. Aaron Groth, our family physician, became a bit of a hero at the hospital. Because he had done an EKG when Ronney first became his patient (due to Ronney's dad's health history), he knew immediately that the current EKG showed signs of stress and sent him to the hospital. Ronney never had a heart attack. The "widowmaker" artery was about 90% blocked. If he had suffered a heart attack, it probably would have been fatal.

God gave us a quiet weekend together before surgery. A massive snowstorm prevented driving on the roads; the hospital had to send out humvees to bring nurses into work. So Ronney and I had time together that weekend in a private suite, graciously provided by the hospital. I think we would have been busy with visiting church members if the roads hadn't been closed, so this was a sweet time together. We talked about "what if"s.

Then family and friends flew in to be with me, including Dr. Tim Moore, a cardiothoracic surgeon from Florida who helped us choose Ronney's heart surgeon, Dr. Anspaugh (who God would later use in 2020 to help me as well).

God placed me in just the right job for me to be available to help Ronney recover. In August of 2007, I could not get hired as a dog catcher! The doors to full-time music teaching just were not opening. I was so frustrated. But God had a plan. I finally found a part-time teaching job in North Cincinnati. The Miami Valley Hospital was on the south side of Dayton, so I could work in the mornings and be at the hospital in the afternoon. God knew that I wouldn't be able to handle a full-time job. I so rarely understand His ways and timing, but when I submit, go down His path and then glance back—He was always so right.

There is something about nearly dying that changes a person. You become keenly aware of how fragile life is and how quickly it can be gone. I didn't understand this until I went through it. I only knew that Ronney was different. He looked at life differently. He preached differently. There is a strong awareness of the end. Then his arteries began to clog again, he slowed down, and he began to physically struggle. He had stents put in, and the doctors said that the work done in open heart surgery had closed.

I didn't really understand how close he was to the end (his dad was 60 when he died), but I began to pray that God would not allow him to suffer and take him to heaven instantly.

I'm a Star Trek (and Star Wars) fan. There is a multidimensional chess game that Spock and Captain Kirk play. I've learned that God works in our lives on an infinite-dimensional level. We can't see Him work, but when He makes a move, it is right on so many levels, even when the moves are tough or painful.

In 2009 I began a full-time music teaching position that I grew to love. Multiple choirs, great staff, opportunities to travel with the choirs—it was such a joy.

Then it wasn't. The district decided it needed to reduce the number of music teachers and I was first on the list since I was the newest hire. Somehow, I was peaceful. It had been a wonderful four years—it physically hurts for me to write this because I truly loved that job. It was ripped away. Torn out of my hands. But I told HR as I was meeting to be officially fired, that God had a plan.

And He did.

I was offered an adjunct teaching position at a nearby Christian university, Cedarville, in the worship department (hmmm . . . didn't I graduate with a church music degree?). This was the year that we had Nico in our home and I was able to spend time being his mom (hmmm . . . didn't God know that I would want to spend extra time at home?). That year, a worship professor resigned, so I was offered a contract for one year as they searched for a new worship faculty member (hmmm . . . I would never dream to apply for this position, but God knew in 1981 that this is where my degree would lead). At the end of the year, I was offered the position as assistant professor of worship.

God knew that all these things would one day come together to prepare me for widowhood.

I would have never applied for this opening. I loved teaching music at the high school. I didn't have a doctorate (although I had begun PhD work in Tampa—another story).

"But God"—those are two of my favorite words in the Bible. He works on an infinite-dimensional chess board. Was it controversial for me to change from music education to worship at Baylor? Was it controversial for a female to be a minister of music/worship at my husband's churches? Was it more comfortable for me to be a public school music teacher? Didn't I take a 40% pay cut to teach at a Christian university, and would I have considered applying for it if I hadn't been released? But God knew that all these things would one day come together to prepare me for widowhood.

Tuesday, August 22, 2017, I was finishing up the last day of prep before the start of classes for a new year at Cedarville. The august evening was warm and clear as I drove to Kroger on my way home. I needed a few groceries and grabbed a birthday card for Ronney. We knew that he had a small window to eat supper that night, then he was going to visit a church family.

I had left Kroger and pointed my car home when the phone rang. It was our neighbor, "Susan, you must get home. Ronney was walking and just dropped." I put the flashers on and hit the gas pedal. Minutes later, when I rounded the corner in our neighborhood, it was overwhelming—the number of people and emergency vehicles flashing, our dog barking, a group circled around on the grass. I ran over and was stopped from going to Ronney's side. They were loading him on a stretcher.

I was in shock. I couldn't cry. I just kept saying, "I'm in shock," as the neighbor hugged me. She had seen him jog then get our dog and begin to walk and noticed that he was breathing hard (she was a nurse). Our other neighbor waved to him and turned around. Moments later she heard our dog barking and Ronney was on the ground. A man was walking by, someone our neighbors couldn't identify, who called 9-1-1. Ronney was gone. I touched his arm as they loaded him in the ambulance. They were still working on him, but . . . I knew.

It is still a trigger for me to see an ambulance. They drove off. Our neighbors took care of the dog and walked her home. Schatze was traumatized and never the same. I drove as fast as I could while calling my sister, Ronney's brother, my boss, and the church.

---

*You need to have a strong bedrock when
the storm comes.*

In the hospital, I was taken to a family waiting room in the ER. About ten minutes later I was allowed to go back to his room to see him. There were no cuts or bruises on him except for the machine cutting into him as it tried to resuscitate him. I asked them to stop. The doctors agreed.

The pit. If you are reading this then you, unfortunately, might understand. Whether it comes as a surprise or thru a longer process, when the trauma happens you feel like you are thrown into a pit. It is black, confusing, scary, foggy, deep, and frantic. You want out. You panic. Sometimes you claw at it. Sometimes you just quit and weep. You lean. You flail. You shake. You wait.

The work of grief.
I didn't know that there was work to do.
The first week is so crazy trying to make decisions.
The stress from trauma.
The fog
You need to have a strong bedrock when the storm comes
The miracle of grass . . .

The next day I was walking Schatze in our neighborhood. I was exhausted, confused, dreading the walk past the ground where Ronney died, but that was the only route. I was at the bottom of the hill getting ready to make that walk when the Holy Spirit entered my foggy mind. He showed me the miracle of the grass. You see, our neighborhood walk was sidewalk, then a few yards of grass before you step out onto a road. Ronney died on that grass. He was 6'5" with a long stride.

The Lord instantaneously (answering my prayer) took him to heaven just as Ronney was walking in the grass for those few steps. "Susan, I'll be just as intentional, specific and perfect as I take care of you," He whispered. "Trust and obey."

I sobbed.

What a blessing. What a picture of God's perfection. What a gift of love—the grass.

The Lord is my shepherd, and all my years of learning to trust His plans and timing were brought together in that instant as He revealed the beautiful picture of his care for Ronney and for me. The Master took care of Ronney. He didn't linger in the suffering. He didn't continue to fight a body that was fading. No more attacks by grumbling church members. The Master would also take care of me.

"Susan, I'll be just as intentional, specific and perfect as I take care of you," He whispered.
"Trust and obey."

Several songs began to play in my head: "Just thinking of stepping on shores and finding it heaven! Of touching a hand—and finding it God's! Of breathing new air—and finding it celestial! Of waking up in glory—and finding it home!"

What a thought. Ronney breathed the air of heaven from the soft grass.

There isn't a memorial where he died. It's a neighbor's yard. But God knew that it was going to be the perfect spot when God moved us to Fairborn.

God knew that I needed to be working at Cedarville University when He took Ronney home. This Christian university showed me the embodiment of God's love that even our church family couldn't figure out. The university gave me time, support, patience, care, cards, anything that I needed and a month to begin to figure out the pit. God knew. He had brought me to this place.

I have learned that His path isn't fully visible, but it lights up step by obedient step—even when you don't understand. Build upon the bedrock of Bible study, prayer, church attendance, Christian fellowship, and church membership (more about this in later chapters). It will surprise you—the timing and the task. But He is an infinite-dimensional chess player. It will work.

The church supported me, but the church was also grieving and, honestly, also reeling from their loss. That week, I saw unhealthy moves by men that Ronney didn't trust, who wanted to gain power and control of the church. So I asked the staff and officers of the church to come to my home for a time of prayer and strategy. When the church is vulnerable, the elders must be wise.

Put on the whole armor of God, that you may be able to stand against the wiles of the devil. For we do not wrestle against flesh and blood, but against principalities, against powers, against the rulers of the darkness of this age, against spiritual hosts of wickedness in the heavenly places. Therefore, take up the whole armor of God, that you may be able to withstand in the evil day, and having done all, to stand firm. (Ephesians 6:11–13)

Our bodies were slumped, our eyes red. We cried, talked, and prayed together for the protection of the church. They realized the dangers, made plans, we prayed, and they left. It felt like my final act as their pastor's wife. A kick in the gut.

There really wasn't time to linger in that pain. I had to write an obituary, and then plan a funeral in Ohio and then one in Waco, Texas. I had to buy a cemetery plot and pack.

Press "Pause."

The funeral home had his body ready for me to see it. There were family members at my home, but I wanted to go alone. I took the birthday card that I had bought (we buried him on his birthday) to place in the casket along with his Bible. He didn't like to wear suits, but I knew that he would want to wear his Doctorate of Ministry tie from Southern Seminary and his Martin Luther socks—so he was in a suit. My time alone with him was foggy, unbelievable, and peaceful.

Driving home it hit me—my spiritual umbrella was gone. I sobbed.

Here is where most men get it wrong and what I wish churches would teach. Do you want to have a strong widows' ministry? Then start before the husbands die. Teach them to not only have their affairs in order, but to also have a spiritual umbrella ready to help the widow, because the decisions they must make will be withering. It breaks my heart how overwhelming and fragile the first days of widowhood are. It also breaks God's heart. Read the Scriptures —God particularly watches over widows and orphans.

Ronney was ready. He was ready spiritually—there will be many in heaven because of his sharing of the gospel. He was ready as a husband. The insurance and instructions were quickly found. He had a spiritual umbrella ready for me.

Enter my spiritual umbrella—Todd Phillips. He was a deacon at our church in Houston and our families were joined together in love for one another and their daughter Abbey (our spiritual goddaughter). Ronney had asked him to be my guide if anything should happen to him. I don't know when he set this up, but it was the most important thing he could have done for me.

Trauma does terrible things to your mind, body, emotions, spirit. You are so vulnerable and yet you are thrown into a whirlwind of decisions. You might be like me and not overseen the household finances and maintenance. Once a year, Ronney would get me to pay the bills; that was basically it. So, having Todd immediately ready to give me advice and listen to my ideas was incredibly helpful. They lived far away, but they came to both services and he gave the eulogy in Ohio and preached in Texas. They were there. Todd, with Karen's blessing, was my new spiritual umbrella/brother. Selah.

Press "Play."

There were two viewings in Ohio and a service. Hundreds came to pay their respects and the gospel was shared. We even had Ronney preach just a wee bit by playing part of his sermon on "Finishing Faithful." While the family was there, I asked them to go through Ronney's library (thousands of books), so they could take some home; I had already chosen mine. The church would graciously give me two months to clear out his office.

Even as I sent Schatze home with my sister Carolyn, I knew that I wanted my mom to live with me that fall. It would be good to have someone in the house even though I would have to spend my time taking care of her. I flew to Texas for Ronney's service and burial.

It turned out to be a difficult time for everyone to attend because a hurricane had come ashore, but plans got worked out and the service was a blessing. Dr. Tim Moore gave the eulogy and Todd preached. It was good to be with the Plemons family. Instead of singing "Happy Birthday," we sang "I'll Fly Away" and released burnt orange balloons into the blue Waco sky as we stood by his grave on his fifty-fifth birthday.

I had reached out to Nico, our German son, and instinctively knew that I needed to see him, and I also needed to be in a different place for Christmas. So, with his family's blessing, I bought my ticket to visit Nico for Christmas, then flew home.

God takes care of the widow. I had no idea what would come next.

I had to drive to Nashville and fly from there to Florida to get my mom because upon returning to Nashville, I needed to take Schatze home. I flew to Orlando. While on the plane, descending into Orlando, I heard someone mention a hurricane off the coast. As soon we touched ground, I turned on my phone and called the airline. I got Mom on a direct flight out on September 8 in the morning and I flew out first thing the next day. My birthday was spent at a Chick-fil-A with family—a somber but grateful reminder of my new reality. The airports immediately began to close after I flew out.

It was hard. It was depressing having a birthday party at the mall. It was scary seeing people sitting on the floors of the airport. But God had prompted me to move fast and get us out. We made it. Hurricane Irma was a category 4 and went right over Mom's city. She would have been terrified.

The services and burial were over. I had my mom and my dog. It was time to go home. I was exhausted, as if every fiber of my life was frayed, but I was seeing God's hand of provision and I set my face toward Ohio and drove.

The Work of Grief

Those who haven't experienced a deep loss don't understand all the layers of grief. I didn't. There are layers of loss that are experienced in years, not just days. People react differently based upon the circumstances, their relationship, and their personalities. Be patient with people. Don't judge. I see so many people get angry and lose their relationships. Grief doesn't come in stages. It is a rollercoaster in the dark, like Space Mountain at Walt Disney World. You can't see what is coming. You just react. One minute life is smooth and even and the next second you are triggered, and the spasms of tears take you on an uncontrollable, emotional ride.

I wanted it to stop.

I wanted to be in control.

I wanted to be in a different place—without triggers.

I wanted to stop hurting.

But I listened.

20

Someone told me not to make big decisions for about a year. I bought books. I listened to sermons. I went to a local widow support group. I attended church although that hurt—the triggers.

So, I dug into the grief. That's my personality. I'd rather rip off the bandaid. If I see that a job needs to be done, I'd rather do it and then enjoy the fun later.

Honestly, I was also impatient. My life was wrapped around my husband's ministry. It determined where I lived, where I went to church, who I hung out with. I knew that I shouldn't make big decisions yet, but when those decisions came I would probably not stay in Fairborn. I wanted to move to Nashville closer to my sister.

So, I dug into the work—clearing out Ronney's office and giving away thousands of books, saving sermon notes, and preserving his recorded sermons on a website (www. ronplemons.com). He was working on the final chapter of his doctorate, and I received word from Dr. Al Mohler at The Southern Baptist Theological Seminary that they would award his doctorate posthumously at the December graduation ceremony. Wow. Todd met us at the seminary for the service, along with a few of my family members and friends.

Dismantling a life: it felt like the scene from *Titanic* when Leonardo DiCaprio is sinking into the freezing water. I had to let him go, with all that it entailed. But—and here is what is important—you are only letting that person go in small, necessary corners of the world—their legal, financial, business, property worlds. When it comes to moving forward (I don't like to say "moving on"), that person is still with you in the form of memories, emotions, pictures, some property or possessions. and the indelible imprints they have made on your life. You are not really letting go, just creating a new way to hold on.

Some people get really caught up in holding onto as many physical possessions of a person as they can. Maybe you have the square footage to do that, but possibly it would be an unhealthy burden to keep everything. I knew that Ronney would not want me to create a memorial library of his books, woodworking tools, guns, all his possessions. I knew it would give him joy to know that they are blessing someone else and not being shut up in a closet to collect dust.

It's the tough work of grief, making these decisions. To say that it is hard is such an understatement, but part of the healing is looking outward to blessing others. I was giving not just to clear out, but to bless others because these were things that I couldn't use. It helps on so many levels to do this work.

I'll go into more detail in the "Splessed" section of this book, but I leaned in deeply for more than two years. Then, in the fall of 2019, I lifted my head.

CHAPTER FOUR

Death...Almost

November 2019, I felt normal. There were times that I didn't think I'd ever get there. The year before, one year after being widowed, I heard the Spirit tell me to stay at Cedarville University. It didn't make me happy because I wanted to move to the bigger city of Nashville, but I surrendered. I asked God if I could at least sell my house in Fairborn and move into the village of Cedarville. He said "yes."

Four months later I sold a home and built a home. Talk about ripping off a bandage.

Moving in the fall meant I was five minutes from work when the snow fell and the nights were dark. What a blessing to be here. I also argued with God about where I would build, but He won and now I know that His plan was perfect.

Spring of 2019 I traveled to Egypt with Cousin Kathy. Life was getting back to normal. I decided to have a big Christmas at my house with my mom, sister, and nephew's family. It was a hectic season capped off with a plumbing leak on Christmas Eve. (Sigh.)

I was exhausted. I flew with my mom back home, then returned with a nasty cough. I went to urgent care and was diagnosed with bronchitis. Fortunately, my nephew's family was living with me at the time, as they were waiting to move into their home.

Three days later I could barely walk. I tried to log into my computer to have a session with a doctor because I knew I couldn't make it inside a clinic. I was so weak that I was crawling to the bathroom. My nephew's wife Ashley knocked on my door and said she would take me to the clinic. It was a miracle she was home because my nephew is a pastor and she normally would not be home on a Sunday; however, she was watching a sick child (actually, Nathan wasn't sick—God was watching over me).

The clinic told me to go straight to the ER. They frantically opened my shirt for the cardio monitor. My blood pressure and heart rate were off the charts. I had double pneumonia with abscess, sepsis, and renal failure.

I was on the precipice of death. Many have died with less.

I laid in the ICU bed gasping to breathe, clutching my purse. Alone and scared—again.

How could this be? Why, God? Everything was going so good. I'm ready to die, but really shocked at your timing.

My coworkers, neighbors, and friends came to pray. My sister and nephew (power of attorney) were called in.

The medical team included Ronney's cardiothoracic surgeon. Dr. Anspaugh didn't usually work at this hospital, but he had been called in that day. God's provision. He remembered me and took such an interest in my case. A nurse told me that when the doctors first met to discuss my case they were amazed—no preexisting conditions. I wasn't even taking any medications.

They put an IV into each arm and began to drop the hammer on fighting this attack. My infectious disease doctor told me that it was a superbug, RSV. Later in the year, we wondered if it was COVID-19, but I went back to the doctor and he said that it wasn't because it hadn't attacked my lungs in the same way.

I went into ICU on Sunday, and Wednesday they moved me into a private room. My sister had come and was with me that week. The next day they sent me home. Let that sink in: Sunday I almost died, and Thursday I was sent home. Somehow God had allowed me to be taken to the brink of death and almost as quickly brought me back to recovery. The last doctor I saw was Dr. Anspaugh as he poked his head into my room before I left: "We didn't do lung surgery. You must get moving."

The clay pot was broken. There wasn't any part of me that was strong as I slumped in the wheelchair and was taken to the entrance to go home. The occupational therapist made sure that all my living area was on the ground floor, or I would have been sent to a rehab facility. I could barely walk. When I arrived home, I found an old cane that had belonged to my grandfather. I shuffled and cried. My body felt like a 100-year-old lived in it. I was wearing a mask before COVID broke out. People stared.

God has the right to touch any part of our lives
at any time He wants to.

Once again, Cedarville University gave me time to heal. Three weeks later I began to go back to limited teaching. I even began facilitating a GriefShare group at church in February (it was supposed to start in January). I was moving and getting stronger.

But I was angry with God. I didn't pray or read my Bible. How could he smash me again? Hadn't I been smashed enough?

Infertility, ministry, widowhood? That wasn't enough?

In his wisdom, my nephew asked to talk with me about what I was thinking. I told him I was angry with God. He said, "Aunt Susan, the truth is that God has the right to touch any part of our lives at any time He wants to." Stunned, I hung my head and couldn't look at him. He was right. God is the boss. He is my King. He is on the throne of my life. He is sovereign, incomprehensible, almighty God.

I surrendered. And the peace that passes understanding began to flood my soul.

Then the world shut down.

CHAPTER FIVE

The Cowboy

To some, the isolation was a balm—you wonderful introverts who relished in the online world and enjoyed staying home. For extroverts like me, COVID-19 isolation was brutal. I couldn't travel, go to work, go to church, or visit my neighbor's home. The GriefShare group struggled to go online.

God had already prepared a place for me here in Cedarville. He knew what I needed. He knew that I needed to be in this neighborhood, in this village of Cedarville, surrounded by people who care. I was teaching online, holding confabs in the yard with neighbors and students, riding my bike, walking, reading, praying and, once again, healing. He knew that I needed to be right here for this moment. Why do I argue with Him?

There were four facilitators with the GriefShare program at church, but I was the organizer. There were several widows, a daughter and four widowers (men) participating in the program—a high number of widowers statistically—but I didn't give any of them extra attention. I really didn't want to cross any lines, since I was a widow.

Pause and go back to November 2019 when I was feeling healed. I had decided that I was open to dating despite my claims early in widowhood that I would never marry again.

However, I knew that online dating wouldn't be a fit and I wasn't aware of anyone in the village that was eligible. So I told God that if he wanted me to date, He would have to send someone to the village.

During the final in-person meeting of GriefShare (now we know), I had struck up a conversation with another leader, Dr. Jim Bijornstadt, about Texas. Rick Troth, an attendee, mentioned that his father attended Dallas Theological Seminary. "So sorry," I said, and turned my back. I really didn't want to engage in a personal conversation with a widower, and Ronney was a graduate of the rival Southwestern Seminary. Jim and I kept talking about Texas. Finally, Rick turned to us and flashed his Texas A&M ring.

"I'm an Aggie."

I felt like God kicked me in the gut.

Remember my spiritual umbrella, Todd? He is an Aggie, and so is my "Goddaughter" Abbey. Rick was driving forty-five minutes from Columbus to attend our sessions. Had God sent an Aggie to the village? Oh, my goodness. God got my attention, and so did Rick.

Rick, being a techie, helped our group go online so we had smooth meetings, and the group even began to watch a movie together on Friday nights remotely. He and I were communicating mostly by email and began to discover so many things in common. We both had "non-negotiable" lists. His father had advised him to create one and I just figured that I hadn't dated in so long, I had better get ready just in case. They all got checked off.

We didn't date during GriefShare; that's not allowed. But we did become friends, and the summer after GriefShare ended we began to date. We married on January 1, 2021. Once we were certain, we moved fast. I guess we had a keen sense of the brevity of life.

Rick and I began to fast and pray that God would work in his adult children's hearts to bring us all together. Of course, they were hurting from losing their mom Marilyn Kay, an East Texas beauty. She had been diagnosed with pancreatic cancer and died five weeks later. What a shock for the family and friends.

God worked. They were gracious and forgiving of our speed. It is amazing.

So now I have two wonderful bonus-children in my life. (It's hard to call them "step," because that sometimes has a negative connotation.) Never did I ever imagine how much I would love them and find such joy being with them. We have discovered common ground in travel, music, deep conversations, and in teasing Rick.

He gives the barren woman a home,
making her the joyous mother of children.
Praise the Lord! (Psalm 113:9)

I am splessed—beyond blessed. I have been smashed. The Potter put the clay back together every time.

I hope you haven't been smashed. But if you have, I want to share some things that I learned that helped me heal. It is work. It is a discipline. But God heals, He brings hope, and He leads to new horizons.

PART II
Splessed

CHAPTER SIX

Start Here

Therefore, if anyone is in Christ, he is a new creation.
The old has passed away; behold, the new has come.
(2 Corinthians 5:17)

Life doesn't usually happen in smooth, easy-to-follow stages. Psychologists can suggest and we can guess, but not every toddler is going to have a "terrible two" year. The same can be said for the recommendations that I am sharing. You probably won't use them in the exact order.

However, you must begin with *surrender*.

Years ago, probably around 1997, I took a small band of youth to Georgia for a fun trip. Our church was without a youth pastor, and I stepped in to help with activities for the youth. The plan was to see an Atlanta Braves game, then go river rafting on the Chattooga River.

When I was researching rafting and the rivers in North Georgia, I read about classes of rapids and, being a person who doesn't like to be sedentary and bored, I thought we could handle Section IV which was known for the Raven's Chute Rapid, Seven-Foot Falls, and Five Falls.

We arrived that morning and had excellent training in how to keep our bones from being broken, how to ride the rapids like you are surfing, and what to do if you fall out. There was also a brief word about some photos that would be taken along the way. We split up into two rafts and headed out on a river that only a few weeks before had taken the life of an adventurer. I began to doubt my decision. But there was no turning back at this point. The youth and adult sponsors had put themselves in my hands, and we all needed to make it down that river.

Surrendering to the rapids and falls in our lives can seem like we are navigating a churning, unforgiving whitewater with rocks below and beside us that can break and bruise. Life can seem unforgiving.

Most of our rafters fell out. I was the only one smiling at the camera when we rounded the bend, and quite a few looked at me afterward like I was crazy (I don't blame them), but when we arrived at the end for a relaxing lunch on the bank of this most unforgiving river there was laughter, rest, play, jumping off a cliff into the river—celebration.

Do you want to go from stressed to splessed?

Do you want to heal?

Do you want hope?

Do you want to discover new horizons?

Surrender.

You must surrender to your Guide—the Holy God, our Heavenly Father—and start the ride. We live in a broken world with rocks that dash, falls that will dump us out and rapids that drive us faster, harder, and dangerously close to death. God sees and He is our guide, but we need to stay in the raft and *surrender* to Him. This is our heavenly Father who said to Moses, "I have surely seen the affliction of my people who are in Egypt and have heard their cry because of their taskmasters.

I know their sufferings, and I have come down to deliver them" (Exodus 3:7–8).

No one has a life with no hurts. This world is broken.

You must start with surrender. Get in the raft with the Guide who sees and knows, and then listen to Him. We didn't survive the Chattooga because of our skills; we survived because we listened to the guides and did what they told us to do. The only injury that day was small—I was hit in the head by an oar that just happened to be in the hands of my young nephew.

Get in the raft. Take the journey from stressed to splessed. Surrender to the Guide who sees your hurts, knows the river, and will deliver you to the peaceful pool for rest.

The LORD is my shepherd; I shall not want.
He makes me lie down in green pastures.
He leads me beside still waters.
He restores my soul. [HEALING]
He leads me in paths of righteousness
for his name's sake.

Even though I walk through the valley of the shadow of death [STRESSED],
I will fear no evil,
for you are with me; [HOPE]
your rod and your staff,
they comfort me.

You prepare a table before me
in the presence of my enemies;
you anoint my head with oil;

my cup overflows [SPLESSED].
Surely goodness and mercy shall follow me
all the days of my life,
and I shall dwell in the house of the LORD *forever.*
[NEW HORIZONS]

CHAPTER SEVEN

Surrender

Trust in the LORD with all your heart, and do not lean on
your own understanding. In all your ways acknowledge
him, and he will make straight your paths.
(Proverbs 3:5–6)

Apparently I began making up words at a young age. We had company and my mom told me to tell them my name. I looked them straight in the eye and declared, "Gootsiroota." It stuck—my family nickname is Gutsie. I think God knew that it would take some guts to walk through this world, so He gave me plenty. I am a stubborn, hotheaded Scottish lass with a penchant for arguing with God. But God is patient and kind. Second Peter 3:9 (KJV) tells us, "The Lord is not slack concerning His promise, as some count slackness, but is longsuffering toward us, not willing that any should perish but that all should come to repentance."

It is my nature to be impatient and angry if my expectations are not fulfilled. But God has a plan, and he has mercy, love, and patience toward us. We can't see the end from the beginning, But God can. That's why the first letter is S: surrender.

"We can have two reactions to God: fist in the air or hands open in the air"—Rev. Bill Troth. I usually begin with stubborn, angry fists in the air. Fortunately, God is patient. We see biblical examples of men and women who wrestled with God, expressed honest grief and anger, and were depressed. They didn't turn their backs on the Creator God; they stayed and wrestled. Surrender can be instantaneous, but for me, it is often a process—a wrestling.

I began to write a journal at the age of 15, and I still occasionally write in it. Usually, I express my honest emotions and that helps me get the stopper of emotions opened up and cleared out. Next, I pause and remember God's goodness and His truth. It is important to settle on gratitude because this helps our emotions to calm and God's truth to settle into our broken hearts. Finally, I surrender into trusting my heavenly Father—"Abba."

I was able to observe Rick[1] as he joined GriefShare with a bucketload of anger that he honestly shared, and then we watched him grow into surrender. Listen to his story:

I have been a Christian since just before my twelfth birthday. For much of that time, I have been fearful . . . fearful of loss.

I grew up in the most prosperous nation on the planet with lots of comforts. Even so, God worked on me and I chose to accept SOME discomfort. But I worried about losing the most precious things.

God loves us. Many friends in my circle like to point out that God accepts us as we are and loves us too much to let us stay that way. Sometimes He lets storms hit if only to nudge us. We say that about OTHER people, those who have trashed their own lives more visibly than we have. But we think we've "gotten it right" and now don't need as much nudge from God. So why should He let tragedy hit US?

Marilyn and I were married for 33 years. We had a good marriage, but we definitely rubbed off each other's rough edges (iron sharpens iron). The worst of my pricklies was probably my anger, but she didn't put up with it. (To say more about that is another story.)

There is no way to accurately describe losing a spouse. For me, it was like my arm got torn away. She was the more organized of the two of us, so I felt adrift. Also, as an "Enneagram 2" I'm all about people and relationships. Suddenly I was alone. But even from the start, God provided.

It was pancreatic cancer. After a month in the hospital (most of it in ICU), her liver started to fail. The doctors let me know. I wrote about it in a hidden web page, putting the link into email. There was a large circle of friends and family supporting us/me, if only by prayer. Two men in particular followed the link and immediately acted. Dennis came over and took care of some really difficult yard work. Scott came up with Jill. She prepared meals for me (which lasted several weeks), while he hung out and let me vent.

And then she was gone. I was angry. Not like the "anger problem," I was mad at God that he had not healed her. I'm not from the Kuhlman school, but I truly believe God heals (here meaning physically). So, I had asked for that. (What else could I do?) But God does not report to me. But it hurt! Eventually there came a fork in the road:

I could stay angry, ferment in my grief, or I could move forward. It was work, but I wanted to heal (here meaning NOT physically). I wound up in TWO GriefShare groups and met with a counselor. Healing takes time, but time itself does not heal. God heals.

Life became a giant question mark. Should I stay at my job? Should I relocate? (The kids had their own places.) Sometimes the questions drained me. Sometimes the aloneness was painful, but the Lord provided. I might get a text or a phone call, or at times it would be the presence of Christ Himself. That was new for me. A new normal emerged.

Along the way I met Susan, an attractive widow with a clear interest in music, who led one of the GriefShare groups. We had many things in common, but I really wanted to get things right, so I tapped five of the men who supported me for advice and guidance. We married on January 1st of 2021. (We wanted to get OUT of 2020.)

This whole saga was hard on my children. Everyone grieves differently and while I had lots of help, the kids were mostly on their own. Susan and Ronney had no children, so it's a blessing now that she has "bonus kids." Chelle and Martin have come to love Susan. We are in a new phase, a new era. We thank the Lord for Marilyn and Ronney; we don't forget. The intersections of lives are amazing, more than I can fit here.

My life now is wonderful. I am often astonished at how sweet things are. Life is hard, but God is good. Many in my circle say that so often that it's almost cliché. But it's true! Life IS hard. But God IS good, and He loves us. The best thing we can do is run TOWARD Him. Surrender. Run to Him when things are bad. Cling to Him when things are good.

Anger will hold you back. Let me suggest right here that if you are breathing, there is something good you can be thankful for. Once I was coaching a widow who had her children and grandchildren living around her, as well as a good church family for support. I asked her if there was anything she could be thankful for and she was so angry with God that she would not admit to any goodness in her life. She couldn't admit the truth because she was angry and stubborn. I've been there. But that anger will hold you back.

Surrender is the falling back, leaning back into God's arms. It says, "I am hurting and angry, but I know that You have my back, You care, and You know what is best. I don't understand it or like it. But I trust You." Until we get to this point it will be difficult to heal and move forward into life.

You should probably read that last paragraph again.

Supplication is falling to our knees and begging God. Surrender is standing up, loving God, and getting in the raft even when the answer is not what we like. It is a discipline that I learned going through infertility treatments. It began to be so difficult every month waiting to see if I was pregnant. We know our cycles. So, I began to say to God, "I love you, God. Even if I am not pregnant." Month after month. It was discipline. Sometimes, actually usually, I was hurting and crying when I said it. I remember one time when I was having lunch with my Mom, sister, and sister-in law. I was on edge because I was waiting to see if I was pregnant. I went to the restroom and there was my answer—not what I wanted. I cried and told God that I loved Him. I couldn't go back to the table and talk about it. It hurt so much. But while I begged Him for a child, I also surrendered to His plan for my life. Year after year, month after month. I was learning to surrender.

Surrender is an act of faith.

Be anxious for nothing, but in everything by prayer and supplication, with thanksgiving, let your requests be made known to God; [ ] and the peace of God, which surpasses all understanding, will guard your hearts and minds through Christ Jesus. (Philippians 4:6–7, NKJV)

Are you hurting, worried, fearful, traumatized? Do you see it? "Surrender" is in the space between "let your requests be made known to God; [surrender,] and the peace of God, which surpasses all understanding, will guard your hearts and minds through Christ Jesus."

Surrender is an act of faith that happens after we beg God, remember His goodness, make our requests, and then leave it there at His feet. Don't wait until you feel it or understand it. We don't have the answers. It is a discipline. When we surrender by faith, He lifts us up and we have a peace that is unexplainable. Do you want your heart, the seat of your emotions, to be at peace? *Surrender*.

I'm begging you: don't be stuck in your anger and pride. Surrendering is the beginning of healing. It is the lamb that collapses into the Shepherd's arms so he can be carried. Don't be stubborn (like me) and think you have all of the answers. Don't walk away from the only One that has the power to heal. Listen to the apostle Paul:

For this reason I bow my knees [surrender] to the Father of our Lord Jesus Christ, from whom the whole family in heaven and earth is named, that He would grant you, according to the riches of His glory, to be strengthened with might through His Spirit in the inner man, that Christ may dwell in your hearts through faith; that you, being rooted and grounded in love, may be able to comprehend with all the saints what is the width and length and depth

42

and height—to know the love of Christ which passes knowledge; that you may be filled with all the fullness of God. (Ephesians 3:14–19, NKJV)

Paul began with surrender to the One that can fill you with all the fullness of God. Anything else—walking away from God, people, being a loner—will leave a hungry hole in your heart.

If you have never surrendered your heart to the One who died in your place for the forgiveness of your sins. That is the first step.

In the beginning, God created a perfect world, filled with beauty and harmony. He made humanity in His image, designed for relationship with Him and entrusted with the care of His creation. But through one act of disobedience, sin entered the world, separating us from God's perfect plan. The brokenness we see in the world today—suffering, pain, and loss—is the result of that fall, as our sin distances us from the love and holiness of our Creator.

Yet God in His boundless love and mercy sent His Son, Jesus Christ, to restore what was lost. Jesus lived a sinless life, died on the cross to take the punishment for our sins, and rose from the dead to conquer death once and for all. Through His sacrifice, we can be forgiven and made new. By turning from our sins and placing our faith in Jesus, we are invited into a restored relationship with God, where healing, hope, and new horizons await us. Will you accept His invitation today and step into the life He designed for you?

Here is a simple prayer that can help you, but the words aren't magical. Say what is in your heart:

Heavenly Father, I come to You today, acknowledging that I am a sinner in need of Your grace and forgiveness. I believe that Jesus died for my sins and rose again, and I ask Him to come into my heart as my Savior and Lord. I turn from my old ways and surrender my life to You, trusting in Your love and mercy. Thank You for saving me and giving me the promise of eternal life—help me to follow You all my days. Amen.

CHAPTER EIGHT

Permission

But we have this treasure in earthen vessels, that the excellence of the power may be of God and not of us.
(2 Corinthians 4:7, NKJV)

I like to look like I have it all together (there, I said it). Clothes are matching, nails groomed, hair is styled—well, unless it's summertime, then I get a little lax. I don't like to look weak. I don't like to *feel* weak. I don't like to ask for help.

Guess what? God uses my weakness even more than He uses my strengths. I'm too self-sufficient when I am feeling strong. I wander away from the Shepherd and start exploring new paths. Pretty soon, I look around and I can't see Him. I've wandered off on my own.

When I was about 7, we were on a family vacation and went to the Tweetsie Railroad theme park. At some point, my parents looked around and couldn't find me. That was 1968. No cell phones. I can't imagine how they felt. The family looked all over the park and finally went into the saloon. There I was singing away, hanging out with the pianist—having a great time. God did make me a musician, after all. We can smile now.

I've always been independent. I relish new adventures. I never grieved infertility. I pushed it down and was only able to cry privately or with Ronney. In ministry, I didn't let church members see how much they hurt me. I'm sure they saw the anger, but not the hurt.

Finally, with widowhood, I was out of control and in the dark. Trauma does that to you. It touches your mind, emotions, body, spirit, soul. I didn't know what was coming or when. I could break down in the grocery store, church, bank, car, home. One night, about a month after Ronney passed, I was quietly sitting at home paying bills. Mom was in the kitchen. I didn't feel stressed. I was just taking care of business. Suddenly my body began to tremble, then shook so strongly that I thought I was having a seizure. I couldn't call out to my mom, but I stumbled back to the bedroom and fell on the bed in a fetal position. I mentally took an inventory—I'm out of control and shaking, but I'm not biting my tongue and my mind is clear. I just laid there until it finally stopped—probably about fifteen minutes, because my mom never came looking for me and didn't know about it until I joined her at the dinner table.

I call it my grief attack. It was scary.

Sometimes grief can feel like your body is being wrung out like a wet towel. Please don't try to stop it or control it because it needs to be expressed. There is a depth to how we process grief that is beyond our ability to control and understand. There aren't stages to grief. It is a rollercoaster in the dark.

Of course, we will react differently based upon the nature of loss, our personalities, and even our age. I became informed about the effects of trauma and learned that some react with hyperarousal (too much energy) and some with hypoarousal (not enough energy, defeated and depressed). I never understood my mom as a widow because she was so different from me. I'm hyper and she is hypo. However, there were days that I became depressed, sluggish, defeated. When those days hit, I gave myself permission to rest, but

I was never clinically depressed. If you cannot function for long periods of time, then you need to see a doctor. Sometimes my wise sister will call me and say, "God told me to remind you to allow yourself to rest." I'm hyper and Carolyn knows it. When I was grieving, I learned to allow for rest, low-key exercise, honest tears, and not allowing others' expectations to control me, but to listen to my body and take care of myself.

The Bible gives us glimpses of grief in Jesus' life as he wept at Lazarus' tomb, cried out to the Father on the cross "My God, my God, why have you forsaken me?", and as his sweat was bloody in the garden. Psalm 78:38–40 (NKJV) reveals God's emotions: "But He, being full of compassion, forgave their iniquity, and did not destroy them. Yes, many a time He turned His anger away, and did not stir up all His wrath; for He remembered that they were but flesh, a breath that passes away and does not come again. How often they provoked Him in the wilderness and grieved Him in the desert!"

I hope reading that Jesus wept and God grieved will give you permission to allow yourself to grieve. It is a natural expression that we have because we are made in the image of almighty God. It is not a sign of weakness, but an expression of love. I sometimes felt pitied and that was hard, but it has been said that we grieve deeply because we love deeply. We grieve because we are created by God and are given the capacity to grieve. Don't let others' presuppositions affect how you express your grief. Maybe they want you to linger longer or maybe they don't want you to cry. People who haven't experienced this level of loss really can't fully understand what it does to your entire being. Give yourself permission to grieve in your own unique way and not according to others' expectations.

It is a natural expression that we have because we are made in the image of almighty God. It is not a sign of weakness, but an expression of love.

How do you give yourself permission to grieve? It starts with understanding that the Bible gives us pictures of lamenting. Biblical lamenting is an honest and raw expression of grief, sorrow, or distress before God, acknowledging both the pain of our circumstances and our deep need for His intervention. In Scripture, lament is a form of prayer that allows us to bring our questions, frustrations, and heartache to God, while still trusting in His goodness and faithfulness. Through lament, we don't hide our emotions or suppress our suffering; instead, we pour them out before God, as seen in the Psalms, Lamentations, and even in Jesus' own words on the cross. Lamenting is not a loss of faith—it's an act of faith that moves us toward healing by turning our hearts toward the One who can bring comfort, understanding, and restoration in the midst of our pain.

When we draw close to God through our pain, we can often draw deeper in our understanding of our heavenly father which can lead to giving ourselves permission to forgive. Dr. Erin Shaw's testimony is a picture of pain leading her to repent, forgive, and draw closer in fellowship with Christ:

When I broke up with my high school boyfriend, my first love, I didn't realize that would be the last guy to show a serious interest in me until much later in my adult years. I am so glad that we do not know our futures. If I had known I would be single in my 40s, I would have melted in a puddle of despair. But . . . I did not melt. The Lord has fulfilled and sustained me in each day, through each trial. While in my early thirties and dating, in my naiveté, I never dreamed I would have another broken heart that would mirror my high school one. This began a dark season of grief and depression. Through this trial, I learned how powerful forgiveness is in the life of a believer. Many times, the Lord has brought me to the story of Joseph when he forgave his brothers to remind me that God is sovereign over my heartaches, and He can use them for His glory.

I had to forgive because even though I was hurting, Jesus forgave me of my sins when I had sinned against him. I have been forgiven of so much, how could I possibly withhold forgiveness to others?

I had to forgive, but I also had to repent.

I had made a person to be my first love before God. Piece by piece God had to untangle my heart's affections. And again, just like in high school, God was calling me to repent of the idols I had made for myself and turn back to Him, alone, as my first love and greatest joy. I often think of story of Ruth, the Moabitess, when she followed Naomi to Bethlehem. Ruth wasn't following a promise of marriage or security, quite the opposite. There was no guarantee an Israelite would marry a foreigner such as herself. Instead, she was following the God of Israel. God alone is our rest and security, not a relationship. That is a lesson that I needed to learn.

I wrote this soon after my heart had healed: *One day my new husband will not be worth all of these years of singleness. Jesus, you are worth it! No man can bear the weight of all my years of disappointment, sighing, sadness, discouragement, and sacrifice. He is not worth it, but you are Jesus. You were worth the sacrifice, still are, still will always be. You are not a consolation prize, you are the prize.*

After my broken heart had begun to heal. I made my resume for the first time in 8 years, not knowing where the Lord would send me. I was asking the Lord for a fresh start, a new way to walk. God had used that broken heart to prepare me to leave what had previously been comfortable. I had my resume for two weeks when I got a phone call from an old seminary mentor. I knew this was the answer to my prayers for what was next. She asked if I would be interested in a job teaching at a university. I sent my resume to her that night. God had given me a whole new life and trajectory. I do not think there is a day that goes by where I haven't thanked the Lord for this new life. I have been teaching for about 10 years now.

In this past decade, I have had two big trials that have challenged my faith anew in trusting God with my singleness. The first trial was caring for my dad after he experienced a massive stroke. He is now disabled and in need of constant care. I am so glad that the job at the university, the one God provided after my broken heart, allows me to be free in the summer to help care for him fulltime. This is the next level of adulting that I feel is rarely talked about: when you are called upon to care for your aging parents. This came to me about 15–20 years sooner than I thought it would. I have longed to walk through this with a partner: to have someone else grieve with me, to have stronger arms than me to lift my dad, to have someone else to think about finances with. A partner is not how God has chosen to provide, but He has provided, and it has been through His church. The church provided countless meals for my family. The church has prayed for my family. The church has been His hands and feet to us.

The second trial I experienced was when I was faced with the reality of being disabled and single. I was standing in the hallway across from some of my colleagues and I could not hear the conversation. I had suddenly gone deaf in my left ear with little to no explanation. I was full of fears of the future—how could I do this on my own? I was not alone. God had to remind me that He was with me and would sustain me. Again, He provided the church. Many people cared for me, prayed for me, fed me, cried with me. Two surgeries later and I have a titanium middle ear with near perfect hearing. The Lord chose to heal my ear, but He was doing more work on my heart. He was tearing me away from my selfishness and developing in me compassion for those who have physical struggles and hidden disabilities.

This is a reflection that came from thinking on Philippians 3:7–11 through these trials: *I would never trade this journey I have been on for a thousand pain free lifetimes because then I would not know Christ like I do—to fellowship with Him in suffering. I would never trade the depth of character He has built in me. I would never trade those nights lying in my bed crying out to God and in His faithfulness, Him meeting me there. I would never trade those moments where I was in the depths of despair, but He met with an unrelenting pursuit.*

Oh, that we would know God in the fellowship of His sufferings, but also in the power of His resurrection that can raise a broken heart, despairing heart and make it whole. He is the prize.[1]

Yes, we are not splessed because of our power, but because of the power of Almighty God working in us. We desperately need God's power as we work through our trauma.

Another aspect of permission is understanding that trauma is deeply distressing or disturbing and can leave lasting scars on our mind, body, and spirit. It disrupts our normal functions and will leave permanent markers in our bodies. The pot is cracked or broken, but it is not worthless. Give yourself permission to value the brokenness. I hated being pitied, but I discovered that my experience with depression and grief has made me a much more sympathetic person. I've always described myself as coming out of the womb laughing and I never understood depression. Now, I can remember how it gripped me and pulled me down, so I can talk with my students who are struggling with depression. Give yourself permission to acknowledge trauma, because it will help you to process and prepare for your reactions.

He draws straight lines with crooked sticks.

One more thing: give yourself permission to have scars. I wanted to finish the work of grief and be the same person again, but being smashed changes you. There were people who told me that I had changed (and I don't think they meant it as a compliment). Well, yeah—I'm living by myself, driving across country by myself and I'm doing it with a different perspective on the frailty of life. I look at each minute differently now—more precious, more driven to be a steward of each moment that I am given because I've learned how quickly life can be gone. I've come to understand my scars, my changes, and even be grateful because it has also drawn me closer to my Shepherd. The drive to wander off is tempered by the comfort that I find from being close. The drive to be perfect is now replaced by a healthy appreciation for my imperfections and learning that God uses our cracks, our imperfections, to show His power. As Ronney used to say, "He draws straight lines with crooked sticks." Give yourself permission to be a crooked stick in God's hands.

CHAPTER NINE

Lean into Truth

Your word is a lamp to my feet and a light to my path.

(Psalm 119:105)

"O be careful little eyes what you see, be careful little eyes what you see. For the Father up above is looking down in love. So, be careful little eyes what you see. O be careful little ears what you hear. . . . O be careful little tongue what you say. . . . O be careful little hands what you do. . . . O be careful little feet where you go. . . . O be careful little heart whom you trust. . . . O be careful little mind what you think."

I felt vulnerable and scared. It was difficult to sleep by myself in a sprawling ranch house in an older neighborhood. I tried installing an alarm system, and it mostly worked . . . sigh. It's like I tried to build up a moat around my life—new car, so I wouldn't have to deal with it breaking down as I drove to Florida . . . auto-pay bills, so I wouldn't have to rely on my memory . . . new house, so I wouldn't have to maintain a big yard and old house . . . new church, so I wouldn't have triggers. . . .

It is normal to go into protect mode after a trauma. You are vulnerable. You might be scared. You might feel alone. You are stressed.

Be careful who you listen to.

Lean into God and let Him guide. Who really knows the river? Who sees the end from the beginning? Who knows you better than anyone? Who loves you so much that he sacrificed His Son for the penalties of your sin?

There are a lot of well-meaning people who will get into your business and want to tell you what to do.

Be careful.

There are so many reactions, but not all will be healthy for you. What will fill up the emptiness inside? This is a critical time for you to make decisions that will repair or retreat, heal or hurt, calm or numb, regulate or overwhelm.

What will you lean into? "Your word is a lamp unto my feet and a light to my path" (Psalm 119:105).

People will want to give you lots of advice, but, "Be careful little ears what you hear." Consider their track record. Are they walking with God? Do they live according to biblical principles? Let me say right here that showing up for a church service does not mean that a person walks with God throughout the week.

This is a critical time for you to make decision that will repair or retreat, heal or hurt, calm or numb, regulate or overwhelm.

This is a great time for you to read a proverb of the day. Whatever the date, that is the proverb you read. You can trust God's Word: "Every word of God is pure; He is a shield to those who put their trust in Him" (Proverbs 30:5, NKJV). Be careful with the advice you receive. What is the motivation of the person and does their advice line up with the word of God?

"Be careful little tongue what you say." Everyone does not need to know your business. What will they do with the information? Will they indiscriminately pass it on (gossip)? Will they pray for you? Are you talking with strangers on Facebook, manicurists, store employees? Some people will prey upon your vulnerability. Please don't trust everyone. I know that you have strong emotions that you want to get out of your system, but this isn't the way. Grab a journal, start writing, and don't leave out the ugly parts. You can always throw away those pages.

The truth of God's provision can become a reality as we lean into Him and see Him working in our lives. Kim Becker's story gives us a portrait of God's loving provision:

In 2006 God placed a calling on my heart to start a national nonprofit organization to help women with cancer smile when they look in the mirror. Hello Gorgeous! provides emotional and physical support to women battling all types of cancer.

My husband and I sold our successful salon and started the nonprofit, which we knew nothing about. I was a hairdresser and Michael had a degree from Purdue University in Pre-Columbian Archeology. The perfect people to start a non-profit for women with cancer, RIGHT? (Can you hear the sarcasm?)

It has truly been a HUGE act of faith.

It's hard to believe that God will show up when you can't see how He will show up. But you know what? He always does. It may not be how you think He will, but he always does.

I had the pleasure of being married to my soulmate, Michael, for 23 3/4 years. I knew that he was the man for me. God made that clear. Our birthdays were one day apart, our front teeth crossed over the same way and we had a scar on our right hand in the same spot.

He was an incredible man. I called him my peaceful warrior. He had a heart of gold and never met a stranger.

Three years into our young marriage, Michael was diagnosed with a liver disease that would now consume our young married life. What should have been filled with date nights and adventures was now filled with doctor appointments, emergency room visits, and hospital stays.

He fought the disease like a champ! There was always a smile on his face and a twinkle in his eye. And no matter how hard his medical journey was, he would always say "I'm the luckiest guy walking!"

The nurses loved taking care of Michael in the hospital. He was just so joyful.

We wrote the end of our love story. Michael would be 96 and I would be 90 and we would succumb to death, holding hands in our red Maserati going 100 miles per hour on the Autobahn.

God had other plans.

I lost Michael at the young age of 56. I was now faced with running our nonprofit alone and making sure that I didn't mess up our son, who was getting ready to start high school at the time of Michael's death. God was faithful and put some amazing people in my life to help me transition into single parenthood.

Two years after Micheal's death, I received another blow. I was diagnosed with cancer. How do you tell your child that his only remaining parent now has cancer? I remember saying to God, "Really, God? Being a widow wasn't enough?" Ironic that my job was to help women with cancer, and now I was one!

Again, by God's grace and a huge support system, we made it through.

Due to the type of cancer that I was diagnosed with, I needed to start a treatment to keep the cancer at bay. It's a shot that must be administered at the hospital once a month. The first shot was scary. I had so many people offer to go with me, just for support, but I felt that I wanted to do this on my own. I wanted to process things and feel my way through this, alone.

The time had arrived for me to head to the hospital and I soon found myself regretting my decision. As I pulled into the parking lot, I was feeling very alone and defeated. I had no choice, I just needed to do this by myself now.

I headed into the hospital, checked in, and headed to the second floor. As I got off the elevator, I rounded the corner and headed down the hallway to the treatment room. At the end of the hallway stood 2 young nurses with their arms open wide and a huge smile on their face.

As I approached the girls they excitedly said "WE REMEMBER YOU!" With tears in my eyes, I said, "You do?" The girls responded by saying they had the privilege of taking care of Michael 7 years earlier on Christmas Day in the hospital. They went on to say what an amazing man he was and how they were inspired by the love that we had for each other. And now, they were going to take care of me! These girls calmed my nerves and walked me through every step of the treatment.

They were such a blessing. Those nurses will never know what that meant to me!

We truly are never alone! God always provides! He always knows what is best for us and makes sure that we are taken care of. He makes a way when we can't see a way! I can say that I am truly Splessed![1]

Lean into the truth of God's Word. He provides, heals, restores, sees, and cares. I began to listen to sermons as I drove or did work around the house. Your foggy brain might not be able to process every word, but it is getting into your mind and heart. Listen to Christian music. Saturate yourself with truth.

When you have a cut on your hand, you don't keep cutting it; you apply ointment to help it heal. You have suffered a trauma. Spending time with unhealthy people or doing unhealthy things will not help you heal. I stopped watching the news because it was stressing me out so much. Be careful.

It isn't easy taking care of yourself and guarding what/who enters your mind. You can ask a friend to be an accountability partner and ask you questions about your decisions. Chapter Thirteen gives more advice about strategically adding Scripture into your life.

I love this duet by Annie Bosko and Vince Gill. It goes to the right person for help. It leans on God:

> These times are heavy
> And oh so dark
> My world is breaking apart
> Lord, won't you lift me
> I'm falling down
> To Your higher ground
>
> Higher ground above all the madness
> Higher ground safe from the sadness
> When I'm weary let my soul be found
> On higher ground[2]

CHAPTER TEN

Emotions

Therefore, gird up the loins of your mind, be sober, and rest your hope fully upon the grace that is to be brought to you at the revelation of Jesus Christ.
(1 Peter 1:13, NKJV)

In 2000 I traveled with the Singing Women of Florida to Switzerland, where we participated in the International Church Music Conference. There were one hundred women in the choir from all backgrounds, mostly volunteer musicians in the churches. As assistant conductor of the choir, I was one of the few who worked full-time in music ministry.

It was a mountaintop experience. Of course, we were in Switzerland surrounded by beautiful mountains, meeting amazing choirs from around the world, and the music was glorious. My roommate and I particularly bonded with the choir from Poland and even enjoyed a quick ride to our hotel on their bus. We were singing, smiling, laughing, and dancing in the streets—literally.

When the conference ended our choir headed to Grindelwald, Switzerland to present a concert. The afternoon before the concert a group of us took a cable car up the mountain to a restaurant for lunch. I can still see the views in my head, the sharp ascent of the Alps above us and the forest below.

I was on a chocolate-and-cheese high. I was also feeling incredibly bloated from all the crusty bread and cheese we had been consuming. We had finished lunch and were sitting back smiling and laughing with each other when I looked down and noticed a path into the forest. It was clearly marked and had gravel on it.

"Eureka! That's the answer to my bloated belly. I'll walk through the woods and back to the hotel," I thought. I desperately needed exercise. I asked the waitress about the path, and she assured me that it went back to the village. I bade my fellow singers farewell and headed out the door.

I wish I could adequately describe the looks on their faces as they watched me through the window. I practically skipped down the path and turned to give them one more wave before the path entered the forest.

Bad idea gets worse.

There was no logic or thought in my decision. I was just propelled by my euphoric emotions and the innate desire to walk off some calories. So, what should I have considered before I traipsed off? Good question! I was wearing slick Keds tennis shoes and a dress. I was alone. This was before cell phones. I had no map, and I was totally clueless about the trail. As soon as the trail led into the forest, the gravel ended and the trail was nothing but mud and going downhill—fast and steep.

Did I turn around?

Another good question. I am stubborn. Once I set my face to do something, I am going to push through to the end. That trait served me well in college and most jobs. On a muddy, steep trail in the Swiss forest, not so much.

I was literally clinging to bushes and trees as I slowly sidestepped. Finally, my brain began to kick in: If I pick up a walking stick that would give me stability, but I also might fall on it and end up impaling my gut. Nope, no stick. How long will this take? How long will I need to be missing from the choir before someone comes to find my dead or maimed body? A long time—hours. Maybe I need a stick to defend myself. Again, no. I sent prayers up and continued to stumble down.

Suddenly I heard voices laughing, shouting, bells ringing. I stepped to the side and kind of hid behind a tree. Coming down the mountain at breakneck speed was a group of hikers—sturdy boots, shorts, backpacks, running and laughing. They must have been hiking in the area and, like me, wanted to take the trail back to the village. I can't imagine what they thought when they saw a thirtyish American woman in a dress with muddy tennis shoes by the side of the trail.

I couldn't ask them to help me. They were gone in seconds. Their feet pounding and laughter in the air.

"Well, at least someone can say they saw me alive on the trail when investigators are trying to find me tonight," I thought.

I was too stubborn to cry, but it was a dejected young woman who cautiously took the next step out onto the muddy trail and continued her descent.

I had made the mistake of being guided by my emotions.

God made us in His image. Let that thought roll through your mind. This *imago Dei* permeates our being. It's not just a subset of a quadrant of our brain. "We are a living, personal, self-conscious, active being with personality . . . a complex unity of soul/spirit body. Man has a will and the ability to select between various choices."[1] We can discern, we are aware, we are logical, and "we have memory, imagination, creativity and language skills."[2] Our designer didn't stop there, but gave us functional, relational, and emotional capabilities. He also gives us the remarkable ability to use these skills simultaneously. For instance, when I was sitting at that restaurant in Grindelwald on a sunny day, overlooking the Alps, I could have logically acknowledged my happy disposition and my need for exercise, but concluded that walking by myself through a forest in a foreign country wasn't the best way to get that exercise.

But I was impulsive. I *am* impulsive. I often let my emotions guide my decisions. That's not their job. We see Jesus, the perfect Son of God, weep and express anger, even question the Father ("Why have you forsaken me?"; Mark 15:34), but we know that Jesus was perfect. Therefore, we know that feeling emotions and asking questions is not sinful.

Like all our gifts from God, it is the abuse and misuse of those gifts that gets us into trouble. I have shared my Swiss hiking story with you not because it is easy for me to master my emotions. I tell you this because many times I have blown it—and when I do, I pay a price. Jon Bloom, of Desiring God Ministries, puts it this way:

> God designed your emotions to be gauges, not guides. They're meant to report to you, not dictate to you. The pattern of your emotions (not every caffeine-induced or sleep-deprived one!) will give you a reading on where your hope is because they are wired into what you believe and value—and how much. That's why emotions like delight (Psalm 37:4), affection (Romans 12:10), fear (Luke 12:5), anger (Psalm 37:8), joy (Psalm 5:11), etc., are so important in the Bible. They reveal what your heart loves, trusts, and fears. At Desiring God, we like to say pleasure is the measure of your treasure, because the emotion of pleasure is a gauge that tells you what you love.

> But because our emotions are wired into our fallen natures as well as into our regenerated natures, sin and Satan have access to them and will use them to try and manipulate us to act faithlessly. That's why our emotional responses to temptation can seem like imperatives (you

must do . . .) rather than indicatives (here's what you're being told). Just remember, that's deceit.

Emotions aren't imperatives; they're not your boss. They're indicatives; they're reports. That's why Paul wrote, *Let not sin therefore reign in your mortal body, to make you obey its passions.* (Romans 6:12).[3]

I also love the illustration from Davey Blackburn that tells us to put the emotions on the train, but at the back. In front of emotions are truth and faith. Many will tell us to deny emotions, and are so fearful of the consequences of being driven by emotions that they reject their capacity to feel. Many will allow emotions to overtake them and control their decisions. Jesus expressed anger and we know that he wept. Since children were attracted to his disposition, I'll bet he had a great smile.

Jesus gives us the healthy picture of emotions being on the train but not driving Him. He set His face toward the cross. This is a picture of self-discipline and determining to do the right thing, even when we don't feel like it.

I will often tell college students, "Do the hard thing. It is usually right and will take you to good places." But one reason why it is hard is because we are fearful and don't feel like doing it. That is natural, but feeling fear doesn't always mean that you should choose not to do it. Use truth and faith (God is with us) to guide your decision, and to help you be aware of the emotions that are at the back of your train.

Do the hard thing. It is usually right and will take you to good places.

Back in the forest in Switzerland, I was in so much trouble because I let my happy emotions and naturally adventurous spirit take me into a dangerous place. Once I got into that terrible spot, I moved slowly, cautiously, methodically, with one foot in front of the other as I prayed. I tried not to make the situation worse. Eventually, I stepped out into a sun-drenched pasture with cows grazing and the amazing sound of bells ringing that were hanging from the cows' collars. I could see the village below, and before I started walking through yards I stretched my arms up to heaven and thanked my heavenly Father for keeping me safe through my unadvised jaunt.

Where are you? Have you let your emotions drive you to impulsive decisions? I've met widows who have bought and sold multiple houses in the first years of widowhood—searching for stability but not finding it, because emotions are churning. Like me, do you need to learn to discern emotions, but not let them guide your decisions? Do you need to do a hard thing that you have dreaded, but the dark feelings lead you to avoid doing it and cause you to be stuck in your trauma? Are you stuck in the emotion of regret? I was in a group counseling session and heard these wise words, "Regret is a cul-de-sac. It keeps us from moving forward." My private counselor taught me (thank you, God, for Christian counselors) that everything that I regret could change and the results would probably be the same. There is no guarantee. You need to move through regret with truth and faith. Put emotion at the back of the train where it belongs.

Emotions are a good gift from God. We can honor him with our emotions, but like all of God's good gifts—they can also be twisted by sin and misused. I like the picture God gives us in 1 Peter 1:13 (NKJV): "Therefore, gird up the loins of your mind, be sober, and rest your hope fully upon the grace that is to be brought to you at the revelation of Jesus Christ." When we "gird up the loins of our mind," it is a picture of gathering up clothing and tucking it in so you can freely complete a task. Christians are taught to gather our thoughts, discipline our minds, focus on God's grace, and be ready for kingdom action.

Brian Hanson has a touching parental story about holding on to truth and faith despite painful questioning:

> It had been a long day of meetings, and I had just finished holding a chapel with an area sports team. God was so good, and things were rolling smoothly as I was able to see the good hand of God upon my ministry and life.
>
> Exhausted by all the activities of the day, my wife and I said our goodnights to the kids and made our way to the bedroom. After the evening routine of brushing my teeth and putting on shorts, I made my way to the bed and saw an envelope on my pillow, addressed to "Dad." One never knows what to anticipate when this kind of thing happens. Will it be good and life-giving or will it be painful and the start of a new chapter? As my wife and I sat on the edge of our bed, one of our children had taken the time to put into writing something they were struggling with on a deeply personal basis. It was not something we were prepared for or that we saw coming.
>
> We sat together, with our feet off the side of the bed. We read the 4-page letter and hinged upon every word written. As we read further, our heads sunk as our hearts sank. It was the type of letter that would begin a new chapter in our lives. One that would take us places into our spirit that we didn't know existed. These were the types of issues that other families dealt with. Not our own. . . .

Although I have had some difficult things occur in my life, nothing jolted me like that letter on that evening. I was shaken. I was numb. I felt weak and helpless, and I needed wisdom that I did not have. How would I respond to my child? Was I a failure? How could this happen in my house?

I walked down the hall to the room of my child not knowing what I would face. Were they angry at me? Would they despise me? Did they want to listen to me? Would any words even come out of my mouth? So many questions that were unknown and would be discovered as the moment, days, weeks and years were to play out. As I knocked on the door and walked into the bedroom. . . . I stood there watching my child sobbing, shaking and frightened by what my reaction might be to the situation they found themself in.

Not knowing what to do, I softly reached down and gently wrapped my hand around their elbow and tenderly pulled them up into my arms. That is a moment that I will never forget. It was perhaps one of the lowest points in my life and yet I will never forget that hug. It was ground zero and a place to build on.

Through much prayer, for years . . . I have watched this child of ours struggle. They have had real trials, and they had to make a crucial decision. They had to ask the question, "Will I own this faith that I claimed as a young child or will I turn away and find my own path?" Those questions are what take us to the core of who we are and helps us determine who we will be.

Although their journey is still being written, I must tell you that it has been an absolute joy to watch this dear family member choose what is right. To hold onto God even when He didn't seem present. To cheer them on in the good times and to weep with them during the difficult times. But for now, for this situation, my heart is blessed. It overflows and I thank God for His goodness in the life of my child.[4]

This story is a picture of trusting God's truth as you open the door on an emotional situation. We need to gather up emotional thoughts and put truth and faith at the front of the train. The lyrics of "I Set My Hope (Hymn for a Deconstructing Friend)" by Keith and Kristyn Getty, Matt Boswell, and Matt Papa are a great picture of this spiritual discipline:

> When this life of trials tests my faith
> I set my hope on Jesus
> When the questions come and doubts remain
> I set my hope on Jesus
> For the deepest wounds that time won't heal
> There's a joy that runs still deeper
> There's a truth that's more than all I feel
> I set my hope on Jesus
>
> I set my hope on Jesus
> My rock, my only trust
> Who set His heart upon me first
> I set my hope on Jesus
>
> Though I falter in this war with sin
> I set my hope on Jesus
> When I fail the fight and sink within
> I set my hope on Jesus
> Though the same would drown me in its sea
> And I dread the waves of justice

I will cast my life on Calvary
I set my hope on Jesus

Though the world called me to leave my Lord
I set my hope on Jesus
Though it offer all its vain rewards
I set my hope on Jesus
Though this heart of mine is prone to stray
Give me grace enough to finish
'Til I worship on that final day
I set my hope on Jesus[5]

Truth—God gave us emotions. The book of Psalms is full of emotional expressions. But emotions are at the back of the train of our lives—the caboose. We will run off the rails, or end up alone in a dark forest, when we let our emotions run our lives.

This leads us to the next part of "splessed": How do you listen to God?

CHAPTER ELEVEN

Still Small Voice

Be still, and know that I am God.
(Psalm 46:10a)

There is constant noise in my ear. Tinnitus. For 99.9% of the time, I don't pay attention to it because there is so much going on around me. It's when I'm quiet that I notice it.

This is a great picture of my relationship with Christ. He is always with me, part of everything I am and do, but often I don't really notice Him until I am still. I'm pretty good about having a quiet time in the morning, but it is planned and I am disciplined about not lingering because I have to go to work. I can read the Bible, discuss it with my husband, then kneel in prayer, but I haven't really stopped and listened.

I already shared that I am a hyper person. My reaction to the trauma of widowhood was to be frenetic; I wanted to fix my life quickly. Trauma doesn't work that way. It's not on my time schedule.

I'm so glad that I listened to people who said, "Wait a year before you make any big decisions." That was hard. However, I spent that year doing the work of grief—weeping, journaling, seeing a counselor, reading books, deciding what to do with Ronney's stuff, and investigating my options.

Option 1 was my favorite: move to Nashville to live close to my sister's family. Nashville is Music City (love it), I love their church, and I love them. I was looking at houses there, but I couldn't find a job despite numerous friends helping.

Option 2 was moving to Florida to live close to my brother's family. I love them and their church too, but I've never loved the Florida climate and it really doesn't love my hair!

Option 3 was to stay alone in Ohio and keep my job, but to move to a new home closer to campus. As much as I love my job, this was my least favorite option because I was alone and a Southern girl at heart. I wanted to go south.

Eleven months after Ronney passed, I was back in Ohio getting ready for the new school year. I was pensive and quietly driving the neighborhoods around the university. I felt lost and alone. I pulled into a new neighborhood and parked.

Silence. "I didn't just move you to the university for then, I moved you for now. I want you to stay," came the still small voice from God. Wow. I remembered how crazy it was that I had this job. He had moved some mountains to get me here and I loved it.

I sat still and soaked it in amidst the late summer sun and the corn fields swaying in the breeze.

I was remembering God's faithfulness.

"OK," I said to God "Can I move to a new home close to campus?" He confirmed that I could, and four months later I had sold my home and moved into a new one that I finished building.

God doesn't usually talk to me like that, but when this widow needed special directions, the Holy Spirit would speak into my still, quiet moments. There were only about three times I can remember that happening. The last time came the following week.

This neighborhood is new homes, and I was trying to figure out which lot to buy. I had already decided on a house plan; it was one they were currently building as a "spec home" on a lot. One night, my senior adult dog woke up to go outside. That never happened. I couldn't go back to sleep, and I heard that voice telling me to buy the spec home. "But I hate the lot that it's on. It has a terrible backyard," I argued. I kept arguing with God until I got smart (and really tired). "Fine. I'll buy it," I said, and went back to sleep.

The next day, I bought it and let go of the lot I had already purchased, intending to build that house plan on a bigger lot. It's funny, but it's not. God was so right! I love the location of my home. I used the savings to landscape the "inferior" yard. God knew right where I needed to be. Because I bought it after it had been started, I didn't have to move into storage, so this home was completed and my house sold at the same time. And this tiny backyard has turned out to be ideal for hosting students, friends, and family.

God knew.

I'm glad that He cares so much for widows.

I'm glad He has a plan for me that is so much better than I could imagine.

I'm glad that I did what He told me to do.

If I had moved away, I wouldn't have been given my wonderful husband and bonus children. If I had moved away, I would have missed out on the wonderful college students I have known and loved. If I had moved away, I would have missed the special comradery of this neighborhood.

Find time to be still.

We were in Great Smoky Mountains National Park, walking down the Clingman's Dome trail. It is a beautiful, paved path that takes you up to a lookout. It also crosses the Appalachian Trail, so coming back down we thought it would be fun to walk a bit of the trail. We hadn't gone far when we were enveloped by the tall trees and the sound changed.

It was quiet.

We stopped, whispered, pointed, listened, prayed.

I looked up at Rick and said, "Still, small voice."

"Huh?"

"It's the double 's' in 'splessed.' That's what God wants it to be. That's what I need to share."

He smiled. We stayed a bit, prayed, and listened to the birds and the breeze in the trees.

Do you remember Elijah? He had been in a massive spiritual battle with the forces of darkness that embodied evil prophets of Baal. There had been a severe famine and no rain. Elijah confronted the evil in government and religion while representing Almighty God. The rain was coming, and Elijah ran (faster than King Ahab's chariot), but the wicked queen threatened his life, so he kept running until he found himself alone in the wilderness. He wanted to die.

Did you read that?

He wanted to die! The Holy Bible doesn't mask our weakness or deny it, or even expect that God's servants are never weak.

Elijah was spent—physically, emotionally, spiritually exhausted and hurting.

God sent an angel to feed him. Then he went 40 days and nights and traveled to Mount Horeb to a cave.

He began to talk to God and God told him to stand on the mountain before God. Then God sent a great wind, an earthquake, and a fire, but God was not in the Big. "And after the earthquake a fire, but the LORD was not in the fire. And after the fire the sound of a low whisper. And when Elijah heard it, he wrapped his face in his cloak and went out and stood at the entrance of the cave. And behold, there came a voice to him and said, 'What are you doing here, Elijah?'" (1 Kings 19:12–13).

The still, small voice.

*When God is your source and He is the center of
your life, then you will not be moved—
even when life around you is swirling with chaos.*

You need to find a place where you can be still and listen.

I understand. You are hurting, and if you stop and stay still you will feel the hurt even more. You will be so aware. I don't like to be quiet and notice the tinnitus. I didn't like to stop and let the hurt rise up. I wanted to keep moving. Stay busy.

But if I had, I would have missed God's plan: where I am now—this good place—this place of "splessed." I listened to God's voice and did what He wanted. This wasn't my plan. This wasn't anyone's plan for me. But I can look back and say that following God's plan has led me to good places, where my cup runs over. Beyond blessed . . . splessed.

It wasn't what I expected to do.

But it was the right thing.

Listen to God.

Be still and know that I am God.

This has been a hard year for my family. My nephew became entangled in legal drugs during COVID-19 and committed suicide. My husband and I dropped everything and drove through the night to be with Carolyn and Ross as soon as we heard. We have leaned into being there for them through our presence and phone calls. It has been amazing to watch God begin the process of restoration as they have leaned into Him.

When people ask me how they are doing, I will say, "They are grieving well. They are grieving with hope."

The two of them went on a short vacation to Niagara Falls this week and there, among the beauty and majesty of God's creation, Carolyn sent this text to the family:

I had a breakthrough this week regarding how I am doing. People ask me that and many times I don't know how to respond. This week I was able to identify where I'm at. This is what I came up with: I'm stronger since his death, but I'm also more fragile and I live between those two. Sometimes I'm stronger and I'm functioning and participating in life. When I'm more fragile I don't want to leave the house, and I just want to stay in bed. So, when you ask me and I say I'm more fragile it's because I've been triggered, I'm crying or I'm angry or something else. When I'm stronger I'm remembering the promises of God and coping with life. When I'm more fragile I covet your prayers. I still miss Stephen every day and think about him every day.

Do you know where you are at?
Do you need to take time to hear God's still, small voice?
Do you need to be still and know that He is God?
Do you need refuge? Do you need strength? Be still.
Do you need God's help in your trouble? Be still.
Do you need to trust and not fear? Be still.
Are you in the midst of mountain-moving chaos?
Be still.
God is our source of streams of blessing.

When God is your source and He is in the center of your life, then you will not be moved—even when life around you is swirling with chaos.

Do you want God to help you? He will. Be still.

His voice is powerful. He utters his voice, and the earth melts.

Who is with you? I might have held my sister as we cried, but the most important presence in her life was the Lord of Hosts. He has all power at His disposal to move and work in her heart and life. His power brings peace, wins wars, and burns chariots with fire.

Perhaps, like Kary Oberbrunner, you need to take your Bible and find a large rock:

After school one afternoon, I hopped into my parents' vehicle for the half-hour trip home. Dad passed me a rather plain-looking white envelope with my name handwritten across the front.

"What's this?" I asked.

"I'm not sure. Your mother gave it to me."

I carelessly tore open the envelope and clumsily unfolded the somewhat rigid stationery. To my surprise, inside were a few pages of lined paper—and some cold hard cash! I counted the stack of bills and then turned to the letter, intrigued with the anonymous author.

Kary,

You don't know me or my wife and I must admit, I don't normally write letters to strangers, but something rather strange happened to me the other day. You see your mom works with my wife JoAnne at Marshalls. She was telling JoAnne about how you went through a series of trials lately: the stolen bike and the assault in the alley.

JoAnne relayed your story to me over dinner the other day. Kary, I'm telling you God spoke to me. In that moment he told me with unmistakable clarity, "Carl you need to encourage this young man." In my whole life God never told me anything that clearly. I shook it off at first, but then the message came back even stronger, "Carl, I can't afford to have Kary discouraged. I need him and you need to encourage him."

I knew I had to listen. So I am giving you this money in order for you to buy a new bike. I am convinced that God has great plans for you. Don't ever doubt this and don't be discouraged.

God needs you, Kary!

Carl Muenzmaier

Perplexed, I looked up from the letter, struggling to quantify my unbelief. "God needs me?" I whispered—half-mocking, but also half-hoping.

Moments before I had questioned if God even knew I existed, and now a stranger just informed me that God couldn't afford to have me discouraged? A large part of me didn't want to accept what I had just read—I couldn't take another disappointment or broken dream.

Still, I couldn't shake it. God had just shown up and given me a significant message.

And I wondered—what if that message was true?

Up until Jacob's dream, God was someone he only knew from afar. Then all of a sudden, God showed up with a message, promising him seven gifts in the form of seven "I will" statements.

Right after God's unconditional promises were heaped high upon his future—ranging from descendants to land—Jacob responded with his own promises wrapped in performance.

He couldn't deal with "Grace," so he quickly interrupted her, shifting the mood and slanting the entire supernatural experience into one big business transaction.

> Then Jacob made a vow, saying, "If God will be with me and will watch over me on this journey I am taking and will give me food to eat and clothes to wear so that I return safely to my father's house, then the Lord will be my God and this stone that I have set up as a pillar will be God's house, and of all that you give me I will give you a tenth." (Genesis 28:20–22, NIV)

Jacob rained on Grace's parade by promising to pay her off if she came through. And while on the subject, Jacob promised a lousy payoff. What could he possibly give God that he didn't already own?

Jacob was in no position to bargain, either. Remember, he had a cold stone in place of a pillow and a fat zero in place of a wallet. Unemployed at the moment, how could he give God a tenth of anything? Old patterns are hard to break, however, and Jacob's reply revealed that he was still miles away from receiving his Secret Name.

Jacob—unwilling to abandon his wheeling-and-dealing posture, even with someone as impressive as God—needed a lesson in economic etiquette. Thankfully, God didn't allow Jacob to pay off Grace.

Up until then, I only knew God from afar, but overnight, God now had my attention.

Shortly after receiving Carl's letter, I drove through downtown Milwaukee, parked the car, grabbed my Bible and my journal, and headed to the large white rocks that outlined the lakeshore. If God had any intention of additional information, I now sat poised and ready to hear him.

Propped up on the rocks, I made a makeshift altar— my attention fully directed to the Bible and the strange letter from the strange man spread out before me. With a somewhat bustling pace, I turned the crinkly pages of Scripture, hoping for more clarity. After a few minutes, I stumbled upon a portion from a prophet named Jeremiah. Evidently, he wanted to remind his readers that God hadn't forgotten them or their situation.

His inspirational ideas seemed consistent with Carl's letter. Excitedly, my eyes scanned both documents at a hurried pace, picking up on a unique pattern. Replacing my heartbreaks with hope, promises suddenly popped off the pages:

1. I can't afford to have you discouraged.
2. I need you.
3. I have big plans for you.
4. "You will call upon me and come and pray to me, and I will listen to you."
5. "You will seek me and find me when you seek me with all your heart."
6. "I will be found by you," declares the Lord, "and will bring you back from captivity."
7. "I will gather you from all the nations and places where I have banished you," declares the Lord, "and will bring you back to the place from which I carried you into exile."

Although intrigued, I was unsure of how to respond to the seven gifts in the form of the seven "I will" statements strewn out before me. With God's unconditional promises heaped high upon my future—ranging from plans to prophecies—I responded with my own promises wrapped in performance.

I told God that if he came through, I'd spend the summer after my senior year as a counselor at a camp. I also vowed to give up any hopes of a wrestling gig in college and head instead to a Bible institute. I even professed a willingness to serve as an overseas missionary in the deepest jungle in New Guinea.

I couldn't deal with Grace either, so I quickly interrupted her, shifting the mood and slanting the entire supernatural experience into one big business transaction. I promised to do my part if God did his. Just like Jacob's response, mine revealed that I too was miles away from receiving my Secret Name.[1]

That is a good word from Kary: receive God's unconditional promises and don't interrupt Grace.
Be STILL and know that I am God.
[Crickets chirping, tinnitus ringing . . . stop time.]
Listen.
Now go outside and look up and say the model prayer:

Our Father who art in heaven, hallowed be your name. Thy kingdom come, thy will be done, on earth as it is in heaven. Give us this day our daily bread, and forgive us our sins, as we forgive those who sin against us. And lead us not into temptation, but deliver us from evil. For thine is the kingdom and the power and the glory forever. Amen. (Matthew 6:9–13, KJV)

If you are like me, then part of the churning in your life is driven by hurts, anger, and bitterness. Whenever I say this model prayer, it helps me to forgive because it reminds me that I'm not perfect—I am a sinner in need of forgiveness by God. This helps me to let go of hurt that others have inflicted—and if I pick back up that whirlwind of hurt, then I say this again and remember that I need to forgive others like God forgives me, over and over.

I ask great things of a great God.

Be still. Stop fighting and let God fight for you.

Listen to his still, small voice. You will know that the voice is his because it will not contradict what is in His Word—the Holy Bible.

I love the book *The Valley of Vision: A Collection of Puritan Prayers & Devotions*. I invite you to meditate on this prayer:

The Great God
O Fountain of All Good, Destroy in me every lofty thought,
Break pride to pieces and scatter it to the winds,
Annihilate each clinging shred of self-righteousness,
Implant in me true lowliness of spirit,
Abase me to self-loathing and self-abhorrence,
Open in me a fount of penitential tears,
Break me, then bind me up;
Thus will my heart be a prepared dwelling for my God;
Then can the Father take up his abode in me,
Then can the blessed Jesus come with healing in his touch,
Then can the Holy Spirit descend in sanctifying grace;
O Holy Trinity, three Persons and one God,
inhabit me a temple consecrated to thy glory.

When thou art present, evil cannot abide;
In thy fellowship is fullness of joy,
Beneath thy smile is peace of conscience,
By thy side no fears disturb, no apprehensions banish rest
of mind,
With thee my heart shall bloom with fragrance;
Make me meet, through repentance, for thine indwelling.
Nothing exceeds thy power,
Nothing is too great for thee to do,
Nothing too good for thee to give.
Infinite is thy might, boundless thy love,
Limitless thy grace, glorious thy saving name.[2]

CHAPTER TWELVE

Endure the

W.O.R.K.

I can do all things through him who strengthens me.
(Philippians 4:13)

The ship reacted to each fresh wave of pressure in a different way. Sometimes she simply quivered briefly as a human being might wince if seized by a single, stabbing pain. Other times she retched in a series of convulsive jerks accompanied by anguished outcries. On these occasions her three masts whipped violently back and forth as the rigging tightened like harpstrings. But most agonizing for the men were the times when she seemed a huge creature suffocating and gasping for breath, her sides heaving against the strangling pressure.[1]

When I read this description about Sir Ernest Shackleton's ship, *Endurance*, being crushed by ice, I was struck by the similarity to how the pain and pressure in life can make us feel. Can you relate? Is the stress of life tearing away at the internal systems in your body? Do you sometimes feel like you barely hope to survive the stress? Is grief wreaking havoc and threatening to drown you in despair?

Don't give up!

Shackleton's voyage on the *Endurance* is one of the most remarkable stories of survival and leadership in history. In 1914, Shackleton set out on the Imperial Trans-Antarctic Expedition, aiming to be the first to cross Antarctica from sea to sea. However, as *Endurance* approached the continent, it became trapped in the thick packed ice of the Weddell Sea. For months, the ship drifted helplessly, locked in the ice, before it was ultimately crushed and sank in November 1915. Shackleton and his crew were left stranded on the floating ice, hundreds of miles from civilization—and one day's journey from their meeting place.

Despite the dire circumstances, Shackleton's leadership ensured that not a single life was lost. He led the crew on an epic journey, first camping on ice floes then making a harrowing voyage in small lifeboats to the uninhabited Elephant Island. Shackleton and a handful of men then set off on an eight-hundred-mile journey across the stormy southern ocean in one of the lifeboats, the *James Caird*, to seek help from a whaling station on South Georgia Island. After incredible hardships, they reached the island and eventually rescued the entire crew. Shackleton's unwavering resolve and commitment to his men are widely celebrated as a testament to courage, resilience, and leadership.

Shackleton's men, despite enduring months of isolation, freezing conditions, and near-starvation, never lost hope, largely due to Shackleton's leadership and their collective resilience. Stranded on the ice and later on the desolate Elephant Island, the crew maintained a sense of purpose by staying active and preparing for rescue, even when survival seemed improbable. Shackleton constantly motivated them, encouraging routines, and fostering optimism. They readied their camp and supplies, believing in Shackleton's promise to return, which he ultimately fulfilled when he led a successful rescue mission, saving every member of the crew.

There are so many reactions to the pain in our lives. There are so many factors that affect our experience: age, personality, faith, circumstances, and many others.

My mom was in her seventies when Dad died. It was renal failure that ended his prison of Alzheimer's. They were best friends and soulmates. She didn't cry much, didn't want to be called a widow, and attempted to have some new normalcy in her life. But her life grew more and more joyless, fearful, and isolated.

It wasn't until I became a widow and shared information from my books, and from my counselor and grief sessions, that she began to do the work to heal. Precious were the times when we would sit on the piano bench and sing together and then begin to cry. I knew that she was allowing the healing.

Yea, though I walk through the valley of the shadow of death . . .

Do you see it? Our pain will cause us to wretch, heave, and shudder. We will fall in the path. But we must get up and walk through the valley. We must endure the work of recovery.

We must work and endure the work to arrive at healing.

I'm not opposed to work. In fact, I'm a bit strange and enjoy yardwork, housework, and being busy. I like to see immediate progress that is tangible, as opposed to my job as a music teacher in which I arrange invisible sounds in the air. I like to see order being brought to a messy house. I know, I'm "different."

There are times when I see work as a challenge to be conquered, times when work is a necessity because I need income, and seasons when the routine is a comfort. Work gives us purpose, identity, hardship, pain, and discipline.

There are jobs that I have loved waking up to do and jobs that I have dreaded. I have had bosses who belittled me and those who encouraged me. I have had jobs that aligned with my talents, and some that were out of my wheelhouse where I constantly felt like a failure. I have prayed to God to move me to different jobs, and I've had jobs that I never wanted to leave but ended up leaving due to life circumstances.

We must work and endure the work to arrive at healing. We do it with hope like Shackleton's crew, believing that God will restore our souls. We do it despite the pain, fear, and vulnerability.

Several years ago, we were leading a small group at church for those with grief. In one of the first weeks, we were discussing how you can get "stuck" in your grief, and a young woman who had lost her boyfriend to a tragic accident became upset. She didn't want to get unstuck. She wanted to be stuck. She never returned to the group after that night.

So, I ask again: What would attract you to work?

I believe that inner brokenness can be repaired. I also believe that it isn't time that repairs. I was talking with a friend who had fallen years before and broken her collarbone, but didn't know it. She never went to a doctor until years later, when the bone was protruding. The doctor asked her when she had broken it, and she remembered the fall. Because she never attended to it, the break had not repaired correctly. All the doctor could do after years of it setting incorrectly was cosmetic surgery to shave the bone.

Don't let your spiritual bones be set wrong.
Take your hurts and brokenness to the Great Physician
who is Jehovah Rapha—the God who heals.

When I felt that I was healed, more than two years after Ronney died, I began to think about the man I might date, and determined that I wanted it to be someone who had done work to heal—not just a man who experienced loss then shouldered through life, but someone who had read a book, gone to see a counselor, joined a group. I wanted the healing to be deeper. I didn't want to be together for a few years and then have the man's unprocessed grief begin to spill out. Sure, our traumas will always have triggers, and we leave room for that to happen, but the healing needed to be set correctly—just like my friend's collarbone.

I have more than a dozen books on grief and healing on my bookshelf. I saw a private Christian counselor, attended group counseling, joined a local widows' meeting, and went through two Christian programs on grief.

Unfortunately, I never processed my infertility: "the barren womb . . . that never says, 'Enough'" (Proverbs 30:16). I just went on with my life . . . until . . . Ronney died and I almost died not long after. Suddenly I found myself with deep groanings, tears, and sorrow that had been buried for decades. It was all rushing to the surface. The wound was never stitched correctly.

Don't let your soul just scab over. Don't let your spiritual bones be set wrong. Take your hurts and brokenness to the Great Physician who is Jehovah-Rapha—the God who heals.

Meditate on the words of this hymn written by Keith and Kristyn Getty, Matt Boswell and Matt Papa, "God of Every Grace":

> O let not this world of sorrows
> Steal my only hope away
> For the power of Your gospel
> Shines within this jar of clay

In affliction, You bring wisdom
That my comforts can displace
How my true and greatest treasure
Is in You, the God of grace
Now to the God of every grace
Who counts my tears, who holds my days
I sing through sorrows, sing with faith
O praise the God of every grace

Weary with the weight I carry
Give me wings of faith to rise
For You know each grief that lingers
Through the watches of the night

Surely, You have borne our sufferings
At the cross took up our pain
And You lead us on to glory
As we trust You, God of grace

Now to the God of every grace
Who counts my tears, who holds my days
I sing through sorrows, sing with faith
O praise the God of every grace

There's a dawning hope before us
That I know is soon to break
As I wait upon Your mercy
Which will swallow every ache

Cries of joy and songs of victory
When we enter heaven's gates
All Your children home together
All with You, the God of grace

Now to the God of every grace

Who counts my tears, who holds my days
I sing through sorrows, sing with faith
O praise the God of every grace

Now to the God of every grace
Who counts my tears, who holds my days
I sing through sorrows, sing with faith
O praise the God of every grace
O praise the God of every grace
O praise the God of every grace

You are stressed, hurt, suffering, and you are reading this book to find the path through to being splessed—healing and hope. I know there is a way through. I know it will be rocky. I know you dread it. I know you don't feel like doing it. I know you feel alone. I know you will stumble. I know you will get distracted. I know you will learn things about yourself and others as you work. I know you will see accomplishment. I know God is with you. I know someone will encourage you. I know the Holy Spirit is your Helper.

Endure the work.

I do not know how long it will take. I do not know how much you will hurt. I do not know how hard it will be for you to begin. I do not know your circumstances.

My favorite worker in the Bible (other than God) is Nehemiah. I've been to Israel, where you can still see glimpses of his work. He had such skills of organization, leadership, and vision. But the first thing he did, when he heard about the condition of Jerusalem, was that he "sat down and wept and mourned for many days; I was fasting and praying before the God of heaven" (Nehemiah 1:4, NKJV).

Nehemiah shows us that our starting place is to weep, grieve, pray, and fast before the God of heaven. He is the source. Our Great Physician. God's name, Jehovah-Rapha, comes from the life of Israel when they needed water to drink, but the waters of Marah were bitter. Sound like your life? The people complained to Moses, so he cried out to God and was told to throw a tree into the water. When Moses did it, the water was made sweet. That is a surprising method, but it worked. Don't doubt the Healer.

Looking back, almost all the plans that Ronney and I discussed in the event he died before me were reasonable and smart. But God did not direct me to do any of them. Had I stubbornly stuck with my plan, I would not be in the sweet place I am in now.

Go to Jehovah-Rapha. Cry out, weep, grieve, then listen to Him and do what he tells you to do.

Look at how the Shepherd works for the sheep in Psalm 23. He makes me like down, he leads, he restores, his presence gives me hope and courage, his protection and discipline comfort me, he cares for me as he anoints with oil and he provides my dwelling. But He also walks with me through the valley of the shadow of death. Not around it, but through it. Not lying down and staying there, but through it.

The LORD is my shepherd; I shall not want.
He makes me lie down in green pastures.
He leads me beside still waters.
He restores my soul. [HEALING]
He leads me in paths of righteousness
for his name's sake.

Even though I walk through the valley of the shadow of
death [STRESSED],
I will fear no evil,
for you are with me; [HOPE]
your rod and your staff,
they comfort me.

94

You prepare a table before me
in the presence of my enemies;
you anoint my head with oil;
my cup overflows [SPLESSED].
Surely goodness and mercy shall follow me
all the days of my life,
and I shall dwell in the house of the LORD forever. [NEW
HORIZONS]

The Shepherd cares for us. We are not alone in the work. That is why the very first step of surrender must happen at the beginning. Our shepherd is steadfast. He is with us. He cares about you.

Whether you are stressed because of loss, because someone hurt you, because you made decisions that resulted in hurt, or because regular life circumstances have caused pain, there is a way through—from stressed to splessed.

We are not alone in the work.

Will staying hurt and stuck in your pain memorialize the loved one that you lost? There are far healthier ways to memorialize your loved one. Rick and I created memorial scholarships, planted trees with Texas markers in the yard, made t-shirt quilts, and we have pictures of Ronney and Marilyn around the house. Sometimes I open the cedar chest and look at the baby clothes I bought forty years ago. I urge you to find healthy ways to honor loved ones.

We don't "go on," but we do go forward and bring our beloveds with us because they are part of who we are and who our family is. When family and friends come to our home, they enjoy seeing the memories. They also enjoy seeing us healthy and happy.

95

I have met people who stay stuck. Who wants to stay stuck? I know you are deeply hurting, but being stuck isn't a healthy place for you to live out your days. It isn't the restoration of Psalm 23.

You can be restored.

The Bible gives us a glimpse of a God who works and rests. He created six days, and then rested on the seventh. We also see that Jesus was purposeful. Luke 9:51 tells us "when the time had come for Him to be received up, that he steadfastly set his face to go to Jerusalem."

Is it time for you to set your face to do the W.O.R.K.? What is the W.O.R.K.? I'm glad you asked.

W—Wake Up to Wellness: Embrace each day with the intention to heal. Start by acknowledging your grief, but also commit to self-care—spiritually, emotionally, and physically. I created a plan for daily Bible study, as well as for weekly physical activity and fun. I reached out to widows, and we began to go out to eat on Friday nights. They were twenty years older than me, but we had fun. In the beginning, I had a trainer come to my home and take me through workouts because I knew that would be the only way I would get activity. Eventually, I took charge of my exercise and would go for hikes and walks.

O—Own Your Journey: Take ownership of your healing process. It's okay to feel lost, but remember that each step you take is a step toward recovery. Let God guide you, and know you have the strength to keep moving forward. There is a phrase I learned: "Do the next thing." My grandmother also said, "You eat an elephant one bite at a time." It can be overwhelming to look at the mountain you need to climb, so just look at the next step. It might be organizing a closet, beginning a discussion about where you will live in five years, or getting help managing your finances. It could be making a plan for a healthy way to memorialize your loved one. Whatever the next thing is, just take that next step on your journey.

Consider Beth Porter's description of the step she took to accept the dark threads in the tapestry of her life:

On February 4, 1973, I learned the definition of loss and grief. My favorite grandmother, Nanny, my dad's mother, died when I was twelve years old. She was traveling from Springdale, Arkansas to Abilene, Texas with family friends when she had a fatal heart attack at the gas station where they had stopped in Stillwater, Oklahoma. I was heartbroken and cried myself to sleep for months. God collected my tears.

On April 24, 1974, my beloved father, James D. Cram, died after a six-year battle with an autoimmune disease. He was forty-two years old. He was my favorite parent. I loved my mother, but I loved and adored my daddy. He called me his shadow. My thirteen-year-old heart was shattered. My mom, also forty-two, was left to care for three daughters aged eighteen, thirteen, and eight. I grieved silently and decided that love equaled death. My two favorite people dead within fourteen months of each other. I decided I would not love anyone, including God. God chuckled.

Grieving both Nanny and Daddy took years. I was young, not equipped or mature enough to handle the trauma I had been handed, and we did not talk about our feelings at home. I was raised in a Christian home and had professed Christ as my Savior at age seven and a half. I talked to God, all the while not understanding why He allowed my favorite people to die. I was angry and hurt. God understood.

With God's patient and abiding love, I came to learn that love equals God, not death. The dark threads of our life's tapestry are as important in our story as the threads of gold and silver. God is love and he knows best.

> My life is but a weaving
> Between my Lord and me,
> I cannot choose the colors
> He worketh steadily.
> Oft times He weaveth sorrow
> And I in foolish pride
> Forget He sees the upper
> And I, the underside.
> Not till the loom is silent
> And the shuttles cease to fly
> Shall God unroll the canvas
> And explain the reason why.
> The dark threads are as needful
> In the Weaver's skillful hand
> As the threads of gold and silver
> In the pattern He has planned.
> —B. M. Franklin[3]

R—Release the Weight: Grief and pain can feel heavy, but surrendering the burden to God allows you to begin to heal. Give yourself permission to release what you cannot control and trust that you're not alone. I have accepted that I will never understand why I wasn't able to have children. I have made peace with the unknown because the strife of constantly fighting to know something that, in my case, can never be explained . . . well, I didn't want to live in that strife. We buried Ronney on his birthday, so we released balloons into the air and sang the hymn, "I'll Fly Away." Think of releasing your pain like those balloons flying away. If it will help, get some balloons and symbolically release them. Let go of the weight—and keep releasing them as the twins of anger and bitterness come back to your heart.

K—Keep the Faith: Even in the darkest moments, lean into your faith. Statistics show us that many people leave their church because of grief. I understand. When I went to church there were so many triggers. I did join a new church, but I never stopped going to church. We need the church, and the people of the church need us. I go to church with a desire to grow in my faith and to help others as the opportunity arises. It won't be easy to walk while alone or hurting, but so worth it. We are made for community. I love the words to the old hymn, "Trust and Obey": "Trust and obey, for there's no other way, to be happy in Jesus, but to trust and obey." Trust that God's plan is at work in your life, and that through endurance, hope will emerge.

Dr. Tim Moore and his wife Carol were dear friends of ours. Ronney performed their wedding ceremony. His story of God working a miracle in his life will encourage you to keep the faith and trust God:

When I was a medical student in North Carolina, my widowed mother was trying to make ends meet with three children in school. To that end, she rented a spare bedroom to a beautiful young local college student. When I came home from school, we fell deeply in love. However, things didn't work out and we parted ways. I went on to be a cardiac surgeon, practicing in Florida.

I did not live a Christian life in my early adulthood, but I came to saving faith in Christ in 1998. I became a serious Christian, and close friends with my pastor [Ron Plemons] and his wife [me!]. Inspired by them, I wrote a book on suffering as seen by a Christian heart surgeon, as well as several articles on the internet. When it was time, God brought me a wonderful Christian wife. My pastor friend married us, and we loved each other deeply. It was the kind of marriage only Christians can know, being in a covenant relationship with God. We had eighteen wonderful years together, but in the fifteenth year she was diagnosed with ovarian cancer. She died two days short of our eighteenth wedding anniversary; I delivered the eulogy at her funeral and posted that on the internet. I had nearly three years to grieve her death before she passed away and struggled for many months afterward. I changed jobs and moved away with my dogs to the Florida panhandle.

I later received a message from a man back in North Carolina I had never met or heard of before, who told me his best friend had died. He had tried to console his friend's widow with my book and writings, and then she told him that she knew me. He reached out to me, and I reached out to her, after forty years. She too, was a Christian. God directed our paths together despite all the decades and hundreds of miles that separated us. We spent hours in the evenings talking about our faith and beliefs. We very much felt that God had orchestrated this reunion through His divine providence, and we married. In a time of deep loneliness and hopelessness, He reached out and divinely worked a miracle in my life.[4]

My friend, your hurt is deep—your faith can be deep because it is in a great God who loves you.. Keep the faith.

Trust God.

Through this W.O.R.K., you'll find healing, hope, and new horizons. Stay the course and endure the work—you are not walking this journey alone. Philippians 4:13 (emphasis added) tells us, "I can do all things *through him* who strengthens me."

CHAPTER THIRTEEN

Discover
H.O.P.E.

For whatever was written in former days was written for
our instruction, that through endurance and through the
encouragement of the Scriptures we might have hope.
(Romans 15:4)

The year 2020 was the year of the frog wars. Oh, I know
what you are thinking: Sweet, little frogs—what harm could
they be? Let's talk about them hiding in the cushions of my
outdoor furniture and then finding the opportune moment
to jump on me. Or jumping up from the rocks around the
patio. They were stealth attackers, the Navy Seals of the
neighborhood creek.

If I was lucky, one of the children from the neighborhood
would be around and I could pay them a dollar to take the
frog across the street to the creek. If not . . . well, the broom
was employed. I didn't want to kill them (too messy), but I
sure did want them out of my backyard and to recover my
peace.

It's funny, I haven't seen a frog in my backyard in over a
year, but I still lift up all of the cushions before I get settled
and have even roped Rick into my paranoia. "Did you check

103

the cushions?" is asked before every settling in. He always says, "Yes," but I wonder, was he thorough . . . and I'm a bit on edge when I sit down (shudders).

Some discoveries are fun, some sweet, and some are frightening. Cookie-dough-cheesecake ice cream! Holding a sloth. Cancer.

What did you discover from your trauma and pain? Did you find a knot in your stomach? Body-breaking sobs? Sudden anger? Dark depression? Brain fog? Panic? Fatigue? Uncontrollable thoughts? Feeling lost? Stress? Hair loss?

Difficult doesn't begin to describe the path you are walking. For most, the reality that you didn't choose this path makes it even more difficult. You are being forced down a trajectory and there isn't a way back to the former normal.

It's like being in a boat about to go over a waterfall. You can grab a branch and hang on, hovering above the current. You can give up and just surrender to the current as it crushes your boat and pushes you under. Or you can build a better boat so you can navigate the waterfall and come out to the other side wet but surviving.

When you are thrown into the raging current of life,
H.O.P.E. is the solid rock when all around us
our lives are falling apart, or the flood is raging.

(By the way, eventually that branch will break, and you *will* go hurtling over the falls. I'm just sayin'.)

How do you build a better boat? How do you create a bedrock in your life, so the storms won't tear down your foundation?

My family was rocked by the death of my nephew this year. He was only 34. When we got the call, Rick and I drove through the night to be with Carolyn and Ross. They welcomed us into their home around 3 am and then we all went to bed. The next morning was Sunday. I can't begin to express how inspired I was by their bedrock. They were sitting on the couch, weeping and worshipping with their church online. Wow. Life with a strong foundation. Here is Carolyn's story:

February 9, 2024 was a day that irrevocably changed me and my family. On that day, my tall, smart, opinionated, debate-loving, great hugger 34-year-old son died by suicide.

How to describe someone who at the very beginning of his life was challenging but worth it? He was born "sunny side up" on April 23, 1989, and since his birth never stopped letting his opinions be known. Stephen was my second son. My firstborn, Grant, was and is still laid back, took long naps, slept through the night at eight weeks, and ate whatever you put in front of him. Then there was Stephen. He took 30–45-minute catnaps, didn't sleep through the night until he was eight to nine months old, and transitions have always been hard for him. At an early age he was diagnosed with ADHD, but he did well in school. We didn't even tell Stephen he had it until he was in high school.

Stephen was also sick quite a bit with constant ear, throat, and sinus infections. When he was six, he had a major ear surgery and not too long after the surgery was diagnosed with an atypical microbacteria. Those were hard times. My husband had lost his job, and I was teaching full-time. Stephen needed to be taken to the doctor every week, and we were down to one car. But God! He provided us with a car. Some dear friends of ours gave us their 1981 diesel 300 Mercedes. It was a tank. We called the car the "silver bullet." Because of that car, Ross was able to take him to the doctor and I continued to teach. For six months Stephen had a pic line with a portable pump attached to the pump. Every day we had to give him six to eight 40–50 ccs of antibiotics. To say it was a scary time was an understatement. We didn't know if the antibiotics would work or the effects of the bacteria on his body. But God! After six months he came off the pic line and had no negative side effects from all that medicine. Only God could have healed him so completely.

Fast-forward to the summer of 2021. I will never forget that summer. Because of the drugs he was using, he was psychotic, depressed, hallucinating, manic and was eventually diagnosed with Bipolar 1. I felt overwhelmed and reacted like a deer in the headlights. At first, we didn't know what the matter with him was. For a while, I thought he was possessed by demons. It was while he was in a mental health facility that summer that he was diagnosed, and we began to understand his drug problems.

For over two years he lived with us and during that time he went to five other facilities mainly for suicidal thoughts. Ross and I were constantly seeking to help Stephen. However, there were so many times we didn't know what to do or say. Our constant prayer during this time was for wisdom and discernment. Over and over God provided what we asked for. We were also learning to trust. I called this time growing my faith muscle.

I wish Stephen had not given up hope, but God has been with us and loving us every step of the way. John 10:26 says, "No one will snatch them out of my hand." I have struggled with the thought, "Is Stephen in heaven?" But God has given me that verse to remind me that though Stephen wasn't living an abundant life in Christ, he was still God's child. Stephen made the decision to follow Christ as a child and he confirmed it as a young adult.

Another example of God's love during this time was would we be able to have an open casket. Because of the manner of Stephen's death, we weren't sure we could have an open casket. But God! Stephen did have a lot of makeup on his face, but we were able to see him one last time.

These last six months have been surreal at times. It's hard to believe he's gone, and I won't see him until I get to heaven, and I grieve. I am very blessed, though, with a husband who has stood by my side, and friends who also know what it's like to lose a child to suicide. For over five years I have also been a part of a Celebrate Recovery group at my church. God knew I would need this many years of recovery to help me grieve and cope.

I miss Stephen every day, but I also know God has not left me, he is not punishing me, and one day I will see Stephen again. Cece Winans has a song that she sings called "Goodness of God" and I believe those words: "All my life you have been faithful. All my life you have been so so good. With every breath that I am able I will sing of the goodness of God."[1]

Carolyn's life was smashed down to her bedrock when Stephen died. H.O.P.E. is the bedrock when you are thrown into the raging current of life. H.O.P.E. is the solid rock when all around us our lives are falling apart, or the flood is raging. H.O.P.E. is the fundamental principle that we establish and never let go of when we are tossed about by life.

I have discovered that my threshold for being crushed in this life doesn't fall below this firm foundation. If you establish other foundations, they are movable—money, family, job, house, health, fun, friends . . . anything else is building your life on the sand. Here is the bedrock that will withstand all that life throws at you.

H—Holy Bible

If I gave you an old, broken, beaten, scratched and burned jewelry box that contained the Hope Diamond inside, would you throw it away because you didn't want the box? Does the damaged container disqualify the gift? Would you listen to someone who instead told you to take a beautiful, pretty box, but inside was a pebble?

Does the damaged container disqualify the gift?

It sounds silly, even inconceivable, that you would reject a 45.52 carat blue diamond for a pebble just because it was delivered in a beaten box. Yet, that is what is happening today as much of our world has rejected the Holy Bible because it is delivered in a broken church.

But doesn't the fact that God chose to deliver his truth through broken people in broken churches show God's love for us just as we are—broken, cracked jars of clay?

The beauty of the Holy Bible stands alone in its perfection. It alone is worthy of our study and fascination. Hold it up to the light and it will shine the warmth of truth into the dark corners of your life. Do you want to be restored? Do you want to be free from the bondage of hurt, anger, bitterness?

"If you abide in My word, you are My disciples indeed. And you shall know the truth, and the truth shall make you free" (John 8:31–32, NKJV).

Shine the warmth of truth into the dark corners of your life.

Consider these five methods for Bible intake and begin to incorporate them into your lives. Yes, you must take it into your mind and let it permeate your heart, soul and spirit—"be transformed by the renewal of your mind" (Romans 12:2).

- *Hearing the Word:* Listening and actively listening—there is a difference. Active listening means you are taking notes and writing down applications. Listen to a sermon as you do other tasks. It is also best to attend church as Hebrews 10:25 (NLT) tells us, "let us not neglect our meeting together, as some people do, but encourage one another, especially now that the day of his return is drawing near." It doesn't say "meet together when you find a perfect congregation"—there isn't one. We all join together just as we are in order to grow, encourage, and serve.
- *Reading the Word:* You can use a plan to read through the Bible in a year or choose books of the Bible. I encourage the use of a study Bible so you will have notes. Reading a Proverb each day is easy because there are thirty-one and you can match the date with the proverb. I like to combine a chapter of Proverbs with a chapter from Psalms, as well. There are also great Bible apps you can utilize.

- *Memorizing the Word:* Choose a verse for the week, write it on a note card, and post it somewhere in your home to remind you. Find a friend to memorize it with, or use an app.
  Studying the Word: I love women's Bible studies, book study groups, and retreats for deeper dives into God's Word. There are online sources for theological certificates as well.
- *Meditating on the Word:* Many of the Puritans considered this to be an essential part of Christian spirituality. It is stopping to dwell on a biblical truth, to ponder it and chew over it until it is internalized and has saturated our heart. You can use your weekly memory verse as the source of your meditations. Consider also Joshua 1:8 (CSB): "This book of instruction must not depart from your mouth; you are to recite [meditate on] it day and night so that you may carefully observe everything written in it. For then you will prosper and succeed in whatever you do." This is our bedrock. No matter the storms of life, these timeless truths endure and prove to be our solid rock.

O—Obedience

"If you are good one day, you will get a Coke." That's what the principal at my preschool told me. I never got that Coke. My mom was teaching a different class, and I wanted to be with her, so I was constantly sneaking out of my classroom and going to hers. Mom had to quit that job.

My poor babysitters. I would lead them on a wild chase and inevitably I'd find a hiding place outside, then double back into the house and lock them out. So sorry.

I took a dead possum to show-and-tell when I was in third grade. The cat dragged it home and I put it in a shoebox and hid it in the bushes. The next morning, I doubled back and got it after Mom finished watching us walk down the street. I don't remember the teacher's face, but I do remember having to take the shoe-boxed possum out to the school's incinerator.

I'm not prone to obedience. I've argued with God. I've gone my own way. However, I have finally learned that He is right. He is true. His ways are not my ways, but are infinitely better. My life is splessed whenever I obey. So many times I have heard people say, "I know what the Bible says, but . . .". This is a problem.

When you get a new toy and must assemble it, you might read the instructions (Rick calls them "destructions"), and you follow them to success. It really makes no sense for me to read the Bible, not follow the truths/instructions, and then wonder why my life has taken a wrong turn. Remember the old hymn: "trust and obey for there's no other way to be happy in Jesus, than to trust and obey."

Don't forget: God's timeless truth goes at the front of your life's train, followed by faith (trust and obey), with emotions as the caboose.

P—Prayer

"Forgive me Lord, for my unforgiveness and critical spirit. Wherever I go, I can go anywhere—as long as You are with me," was my prayer this morning. Then it struck me—the prayer of Moses in Exodus 33:15: "If your presence will not go with me, do not bring us up from here." Rick incorporated it into our wedding service. How do I begin to write about prayer without first confessing that I have struggled to consistently pray? Yes, I do pray, but often I rush ahead without seeking God's face, guidance, and blessing. I've tried to be honest in my writing and share some of those stories, but there are, unfortunately, more that I could share.

In this latter stage of my life, I can set most of my teaching schedule so I begin later in the morning. This has created a wonderful pattern of beginning the day with Rick in the living room drinking coffee, reading the Word, discussing the Word, and praying together.

We also have set aside days for specific fasting and prayer, as well as our private times of prayer.

Without prayer all the other pieces of this restoration puzzle will not reach their ultimate end—life transformation. Prayer is central to the process. The Bible encourages us, "Devote yourselves to prayer; stay alert in it with thanksgiving" (Colossians 4:2, CSB).

- Prayer is a foundational way in which we demonstrate our love for God's people and our devotion to our Heavenly Father.
- Prayer is the main way we demonstrate our concern with glorifying God in our lives.
- Prayer helps us become more Christlike. Jesus is our example of setting aside time for prayer.

Without prayer all the other pieces of this restoration puzzle will not reach their ultimate end —life transformation.

How do you pray?
- A quiet conversation with your Heavenly Father will open the door to *A*doration of God, *C*onfession of sins, *Th*anksgiving, and *S*upplication for your needs and the needs of others. This is called the ACTS method of prayer.
- Take a passage in the Bible, read a verse, meditate on it, and then pray it back to God. For instance, "The Lord is my Shepherd, I shall not want" can lead to, "Thank you, God that you are watching

over me. You know my needs, you know my wants, you are ever vigilant to provide for me, and I love you and trust you."

- Pray with others.
- Pray persistently. *Pray constantly (*1 Thessalonians 5:17).
- Write down prayer requests in your journal with the date you began to pray, and then go back and record the date the prayer was answered (whether or not you like the answer). I have done this since I was 15 and I love going back to remember how God has answered prayers.

You don't have to begin with an hour of prayer. J u s t begin to talk with God and listen to Him.

E—Endurance

Here it is again—that pesky word *endurance*. It just won't leave us alone. Sometimes life is running the race with the wind in our hair and a smile on our face. Sometimes life is putting one foot in front of the other. Sometimes we limp along, with our friend lifting us up.

I love the story of the Olympic runner Derek Redmond; he tore his hamstring, and his father ran out onto the track and helped him limp to the finish line. We need people like that in our lives. And we need to be that person for others.

Do you need endurance? "May the God who gives endurance and encouragement give you the same attitude of mind toward each other that Christ Jesus had" (Romans 15:5, NIV). Our source of strength to endure is Abba. Our Heavenly Father.

I was looking through my stash of memorabilia and found my mother's journal. I forgot that I had it. Thirty-five days before my dad died she wrote these final words:

"Being strengthened with all power according to His glorious might so that I may have great *endurance* and patience and joyfully giving thanks to the Father, who has qualified me to share in the inheritance of the saints in the kingdom of light" (Colossians 1:11–12). This scripture is so special because I realized last night (due to a sermon I heard) that God wants me to have patient endurance in taking care of Mac. "Qualifies" is a special word for us and Jesus has qualified me by His blood to share in the Kingdom of light!

Wow. Tears. She took care of my Dad at home during ten years of Alzheimer's. Weeks after she wrote this in her journal, I was talking to her on the phone, and she sounded so exhausted I was afraid she was about to have a stroke. I got on a plane and headed to Florida, where I was able to help her admit Dad into the hospital, having no idea that he was just days away from graduating to heaven. I came back home and was not there for his passing, but my task was to help her and start the process for his end care. My siblings were there for his final breath.

Looking back (hindsight is always 20/20), we can see how God's timing was gracious and how hard Mom worked to care for him. She endured to the end caring for my dad, and my siblings and I came around her to help her.

I'm grateful for that picture of endurance that I have witnessed. What is it that you need to endure? The work of healing? Caring for a loved one? Difficult jobs? Infertility?

Sometimes I sit down on the trail. The past few days I've been feeling (I know, they should be at the back of the train) discouraged by the number of details still needed in order to finish this book. This morning during our quiet time I was refreshed, and I told Rick that I was ready to climb to the top of this mountain. I set my face to finish. I prayed and thanked God for the encouragement and help. Then I got up and began to write.

Jesus is our picture of endurance: "When the days drew near for him to be taken up, he set his face to go to Jerusalem" (Luke 9:51).

He was not surprised by his future. He knew the task. He knew the battle. He knew the reward (for us). He set his face. You don't have to set your face on the entire mountain. You can set your face on the next part of the trail, then rest a bit. Just keep going up the trail. There is restoration. There are rewards. There is . . .

CHAPTER FOURTEEN

Healing, Hope, and New Horizons

Surely goodness and mercy shall follow me all the days of my life, and I shall dwell in the house of the LORD forever.
(Psalm 23:6)

"Now my life is beautiful . . . praise comes easy to me.
. . ." Rick and I were bonding over our love for music. We discovered that the band Chicago is our favorite (and we've been to three concerts since we married three-and-a-half years ago). One day, he started singing (he does have a beautiful voice):

> Now my life is beautiful;
> praise comes easy to me,
> but I failed when all was darkness
> for the truth was
> so hard to see.
>
> Oh, but, thank you for the trial,
> if it will bring me close to you.
> Help me, Lord, to smile,
> when things don't go

the way I'd want them to.
If I suffer pain, help me,
that I don't complain,
but thank you, Lord, and praise you just the same.
I want to thank you, Lord, and praise you just the same[1]

What? I stopped dead in my tracks. I used to sing that song all the time when I was 16. I loved Evie, the artist who had recorded it. I was amazed that I had sung those words with all my heart and then I had forgotten the message until Rick started singing it.

Holding, guiding, protecting, providing.

The benefit to being in my sixties is the ability to look back down the mountain and have a new perspective on my life—the struggles, valleys, hills, meadows, and heights. Through all of it, I have grown so much closer to Abba as I have clung to Him, looked for Him and always found Him to be here. Holding, guiding, protecting, providing. Just like the song, "thank you for the trial if it will bring me close to you."

The song "The Goodness of God" has a special place in my heart because Rick and I sang it when we were in a boat on the Sea of Galilee, where Peter walked on water. Peter got out of the boat—you have to—if you want to walk on water.

I've been talking about building a better boat, laying down the bedrock of your life, so you can go through the rapids and over the waterfalls when they hit.

Now you are ready to step out of the boat and into new horizons. You have surrendered to God, leaned into His truth, released anger and bitterness, listened to his still, small voice, endured the work, and held onto hope. Now:

What is across the horizon for you?

Who will you help?

Where will God send you?

Is there a storm coming?

Do not fear.

Those three words, "do not fear," show up a lot in the Bible. Why wouldn't we be fearful? We don't know what is out there. We have no idea how we will be hurt again. We don't even know if we will be successful or capable or . . . stop.

Do not fear.

Why?

God is with us.

Step out of the boat and into new horizons.

I hope you have surrendered to Him. He is the Alpha and the Omega. The beginning and the end. He alone can sustain us, deliver us, and restore us. He is with us. It is hard not to be afraid. I must fight it. That's why transforming our minds is so important. He is with us. Do not fear. Step out of the water and you will find that Jesus is already there—walking on it, stretching out His hands to you. See those nail scars in His hands? Take hold of those hands. He will never let you go. His scars are proof of His love and your hope. His healing will lead you to new horizons.

Addendum

Susan's List
Reformed believer
Tither/giver
Travels well
Music lover
Six-day creation
Good with children
Smart
Fun
Kind
Financial Peace University
End-times studies
Salvation story
Pray-er
Missions supporter
Todd interview/approve

Rick's List
Loves the Lord deeply
Prays consistently
Heart for ministry
Loves Chelle and Martin
Likes CCM, gets it
Loves apologetics/theology
Obedient (to the Lord, not a shrinking violet)
Connector to help me
Organized to balance me
Likes travel, esp. nature, hiking, fitness
hiking, fitness

Endnotes

Chapter Four: The Cowboy
1. You can see our list of non-negotiables in the Addendum.

Chapter Seven: Surrender
1. Rick Troth, computer systems engineer, CISSP, amateur radio junkie N5VDC, music aficionado, coffee connoisseur, and new world traveler thanks to Cruizin' Susan.

Chapter Eight: Permission
1. Dr. Erin Shaw is associate professor of women's ministry at Cedarville University in Ohio. She is a member of Centerville Christian Fellowship, where she coordinates the women's ministry.

Chapter Nine: Lean into Truth
1. Kim Becker is Founder of Hello Gorgeous! Of Hope, Inc.
2. Annie Bosko featuring Vince Gill, "Higher Ground," 2024 Tommy Sims/Annie Bosko, https://genius.com/Annie-bosko-higher-ground-lyrics.

Chapter Ten: Emotions
1. John MacArthur and Richard Mayhue, *Biblical Doctrine* (Wheaton, IL: Crossway, 2017), 413–414.
2. Ibid, 414.
3. Jon Bloom, "Your Emotions Are a Gauge, Not a Guide," DesiringGod, August 3, 2012, https://www.desiringgod.org/articles/your-emotions-are-a-gauge-not-a-guide.
4. Brian Hanson is husband to Mandi and father to four wonderful children, a youth pastor for twenty-three years as well as a chaplain to professional and college athletes. He currently is the Director of International Ministries for Capitol Ministries.
5. Keith Getty, Matt Boswell, Matt Papa, "I Set My Hope (Hymn for a Deconstructing Friend)," 2023 Getty Music Publishing (BMI), https://static1.squarespace.com/static/5716a5ea7da24f462d7beeca/t/6500c688ca37057d4c92d125/1694549641349/I+Set+My+Hope+on+Jesus+-+Official+Chord+Charts.pdf.

Chapter Eleven: Still, Small Voice
1. Kary Oberbrunner is a *Wall Street Journal* and *USA Today* bestselling author of more than a dozen books. As CEO of Igniting Souls and Blockchain Life, he helps authors, entrepreneurs, and influencers publish, protect, and promote their intellectual Property and turn it into eighteen streams of income. As a young man, he suffered from severe stuttering, depression, and self-injury. Today a transformed man, Kary ignites souls.
2. Arthur Bennett, ed., *The Valley of Vision, A Collection of Puritan Prayers & Devotions* (Carlisle: The Banner of Truth Trust; Cambridge: Cambridge University Press, 1975), 8–9.

Chapter Twelve: Endure the W.O.R.K.

1. Alfred Lansing, *Endurance* (New York: Basic Books, 2014). 7.
2. Keith Getty, Kristyn Getty, Matt Boswell, and Bryan Fowler, "God of Every Grace," 2023 Getty Music Publishing (BMI), https://genius.com/Keith-and-kristyn-getty-matt-boswell-and-matt-papa-god-of-every-grace-lyrics.
3. Beth Cram Porter lives in Cedarville, Ohio and serves as professor of vocal music and chair of the department of music and worship at Cedarville University. Originally from Texas, Beth is amazed by how much more there is to learn about God and his Word, and is humbled to realize how very much her Abba Father loves her.
4. Dr. Wistar Moore, III (Tim) is a retired Cardiothoracic surgeon, pilot, and restorer of Norden bombsights.

Chapter Thirteen: Discover H.O.P.E.

1. After forty years of teaching, Carolyn Macdonald is retired and enjoying spending time with family and friends. She is active in her church's Celebrate Recovery ministry and enjoys hiking, traveling, and taking naps with her husband!

Chapter Fourteen: Healing, Hope, and New Horizons

1. Evie, "Praise You Just the Same," written by Ron Harris and Shaless Lucas, 1975 Linx Music, https://www.musixmatch.com/lyrics/Evie-2/Praise-You-Just-the-Same.

Dr. Edna Frenchwood, Biography

Edna Chichi Njoku is a driven, passionate, charismatic entertainer, producer, and entrepreneur. She started to venture into the world of stand-up comedy, winning over her audience with her remarkable stage presence and her unique eight voice-over accents and impersonations! Her work on the stage is not just about stand-up comedy: she is a driven singer-songwriter and rapper with an album out, "radio plays", a mix of music and theatricality, where She {Stage name Chichi Stylxz} brilliantly interprets different radio hosts and call- in guests with different accents.

Chichi started Mychichitv in 2009 while studying film and media. She interviewed several artists on her first show "What's Hot in Lansing", such as Wiz Khalifa, Angela Winbush, and Ginuwine to mention a few. Upon finishing her internship at WLNS 6 Lansing, MI, she moved forward with her first love~ films.

Stage work is deeply rooted within the heart and mind of this talented performer, although she loves working behind the scenes as well: she is an indie film producer and actress with 10 films under her belt since 2011. Starting her own film company, Chichimovies, and gained accolades from institutions the likes of the African Oscars (2013 and 2014), 2 Time Dove Award recipient, Indie Merit award, to mention but a few. She has worked with the likes of, Malik Yoba of Empire, Tiny Tommy Lister of Fifth Element and Friday, Micheal Blackson, Terry Cummings, Rodney Perry of Madea's House, Shanica Knowles, Eric Roberts, 2Face Baba, Pascal Atuma, Van Vicker, John Dumelo, Pastsha Bay, Vitalis Ndubisi and more!

In 2014, Seven-time award winning film producer Chichi launched a new network, CHITV {Where Spotlighting you, is exciting TV!}. It vows to spotlight others in their talents, arts, music, shows & films.

In 2015, Chichi launched her comedic late-night show on this network. "The Late Night Show with Chichi Stylxz", interviewing the likes of Ben Bruce of Silverbird, and the Online popular talk show host, Princess Fumi Hancock. The Shows aired on the Comcast Cable Channel 90, in Michigan. CHITV has also added 3 new shows to their lineup in 2016 and aired all 4 shows in over 1 million homes that year.

In 2015, "Of Sentimental Value" signed a worldwide distribution deal with Green Apple Entertainment. In 2016 her Sixth film 'Red Flags', The Final Saga, premiered in Las Vegas! In 2017, ChichiMovies Inc. launched the Mid Michigan Youth Initiative, teaching the youth media and providing jobs. In 2018, the company(INC.) turned 3 and shot its first two short films with the youth! In Feb. 2019 Chichi became a best-selling author of 'Tear the Veil' released at the United Nations.

In 2020, Chichi launched her luxurious redesign bag line, Exotic Afrika by Akwa Eden, which gained prominence in films and fashion shows. During the pandemic, she also engaged audiences with self-care tips through her Late Night TV Show. Around October of that year, she introduced the Flix Reps Festival and Masterclass, a virtual media program aimed at nurturing creative talent.

By 2021 and 2022, Chichi added seven film projects to her portfolio, some of which advanced to production. 'The Terry Cummings Story' production began and Chichi added Ozzie Areu as a lead producer while filming at the Former Tyler Perry Studios. Among her notable achievements was co-directing and producing the international blockbuster Double Dekoi, which created over 30 film industry jobs for her students and staff from Atlanta, Houston, and Michigan.

In 2023, Chichi completed her Master's in Law at Liberty University and was honored with an Honorary Doctorate from CICA International. By the end of the year, Dr. Edna Frenchwood successfully raised $5 million to support the development and casting of key projects, including Tribal Echoes and Rehab My Life TV Show. The finance deal is ongoing with massive press releases pending on the industry partners who have joined.

In early 2024, Dr. Chichi embraced a public relations role, representing a diverse array of prominent figures, including senators and royalty. She made her second appearance at the United Nations, this time accompanied by 13 accomplished women, amplifying their collective voices on a global stage. That same year, she delivered her first TED Talk, titled Pain, Power, and Purpose, which resonated deeply with audiences worldwide. Additionally, her Blockbuster Film 'Double Dekoi', aired at The Infamous Toronto Film Festival. Dr.

Chichi penned an EP contract with the multi-million dollar biopic titled, 'Nasty Girl'- Denise Mathews Story.

Looking ahead, Dr. Chichi is scheduled to speak at two prestigious events in December 2024: the Westminster Palace and the Financial Times with Reputation Poll. At these venues, she will share her insights on international film finance, further solidifying her influence as a thought leader in the intersection of global storytelling and financial innovation.

Chichi attributes all her accomplishments to Christ, family, and mentors!!

Pictures

Nico, Ronney, Abbey, Me, Karen, Todd

Rick, Chelle, Me, Martin

About the Author

Susan Troth is a respected leader in worship ministry who is known for her deep commitment to community service, mentoring the next generations, and helping others navigate personal loss and find healing. After losing her husband, Dr. Ron Plemons, to a heart attack in 2017, she was faced with the dual grief of widowhood and infertility. This profound loss shifted the direction of her life, leading her to focus on helping other women who have experienced similar hardships, offering support through their journey of loss through her coaching ministry, Stressed to Splessed.

In her professional life, Susan has worn many hats, including serving as a worship minister, a pastor's wife, K–12 music teacher, and now as an Associate Professor of Worship at Cedarville University. In December of 2024 she received the Presidential Lifetime Achievement Award for Community Service. In 2021 she was awarded the Cedarville University Service Award. Throughout her career she has volunteered to serve in disaster relief, Red Cross, mission trips around the globe, coaching internationally, leading women's Bible studies, premarital counseling, grief counseling, camp ministry, prison ministry, youth ministry, children's ministry, community hymn sings, choir tours and as a judge for the National American Miss pageant.

Beyond her academic and ministerial work, Susan is a certified guide who is trauma informed, as she supports others dealing with grief and traumatic life experiences. She coaches people where they are - online, in hospitals, restaurants, schools and in their homes.

Susan's life and work stand as a testament to the power of faith and resilience despite trauma and hurt. Her heart for service, especially toward women dealing with the pain of loss, has made her a beacon of hope within the Christian community.

S2S Affinity Group
Stressed to Splessed

SPEAKER   COURSES   COMMUNITY

I'm a Big-hearted Inner-healer who helps women suffering and stressed find healing, hope, and new horizons with my 8-Part S.P.L.E.S.S.E.D. journey of God-partnered restoration (psalm 23)

SUSANTROTH.COM

Find Healing, Hope, and New Horizons

Let's Connect!

Follow me on Instagram

Affinity Group